english sp
spaniel

understanding and
caring for your breed

english springer spaniel

understanding and
caring for your breed

Written by
Marina Brown

Pet Book Publishing Company

The Old Hen House St Martin's Farm, Zeals,
 Warminster,
Wiltshire BA12 6NZ

Printed by Printworks Global Ltd, London & Hong Kong

ISBN: 978-1-910488-41-6

Acknowledgements

The publishers would like to thank the following for help with
photography: Gareth Lawler (Roqfolly) and Ann Corbett (Trinmere)

Contents

Introducing the English Springer Spaniel

The English Springer Spaniel is the oldest of the sporting gundogs, and although he is still highly valued as a working dog, his happy, friendly temperament and biddable disposition have made him a firm favourite among pet owners.

Physical characteristics

A dog of medium size, the English Springer is strong, compact and symmetrical in build. He is the tallest of the land spaniels, and is the most athletic. His working role is to find, flush and retrieve game for the gun, and he does this on land and in water. To carry out these tasks, he needs strength stamina and endurance, which emanate from his well-

proportioned, well-balanced body, with its deep chest and powerful hindquarters.

The Spaniel family, most particularly the English and American Cocker, the Welsh Springer, the Clumber, Field and Sussex Spaniel, have an instantly recognisable head type with a broad, rounded skull, framed by pendulous ears. The eyes are dark hazel and almond-shaped and have an alert, yet kindly expression. As a gundog, hunting for game through thorny undergrowth, working in all weathers, and often called on to swim in freezing water, the English Springer has a coat that offers maximum protection. The outer coat is of medium length and lies close to the body, the undercoat is short, soft and dense.

The ears, chest, legs belly and tail are well feathered. The English Springer comes in four colours: liver and white and black and white are most commonly seen but either of these colour combinations may have tan markings. It was customary to dock the tails of gundogs, and this became the norm for pet dogs. However, legislation has been introduced in most parts of the world, excluding the USA, which outlaws tail docking for English Springers with the exception of working gundogs. The typical full tail of an English Springer is set low and feathered, and has the lively, wagging action that is so typical of the Spaniel family.

Temperament

The English Springer Spaniel has a temperament that is second to none. As a working gundog he is sound and intelligent. His role on the shooting field means he has always had to work closely with his handler and this has given him a friendly, biddable disposition. These characteristics transfer to the role of companion dog, and the English Springer is ideally suited to family life. He loves people – both adults and children – and will be a loyal and affectionate member of the family circle.

Loving, loyal and affectionate, the Springer is an outstanding companion dog.

It is important to be aware that within the breed there are two distinct types: show and working. Sportsmen want a high-energy dog that has the build and athleticism to work in the field. The coat needs to provide protection, but the colour and markings are irrelevant and excessive feathering is a hindrance. In contrast, a show dog needs to present himself to maximum advantage, and an impressive looking dog with a glamorous coat and symmetrical markings is likely to catch the judge's eye. Today a working dog is generally smaller and finer in bone, and his ears are shorter in length and higher set. He will have substantially less feathering and may have more white in his colouring.

The head may also be different with a broader, flatter skull, and a finer muzzle. In terms of temperament, a Springer from working lines will be high in energy and can be excitable and demanding if he does not have sufficient mental stimulation. In contrast, the show dog, along with his more glamorous look, has a more laid back temperament which is far more suitable for pet owners. Unless you have plans to work your English Springer, either in the field or competing in one of the canine sports, you would be strongly advised to choose from a litter produced by a show breeder so you can be sure of getting a dog who will fit in perfectly with your family.

Facing page: An English Springer from working lines looks very different from his show-bred cousin.

Tracing back in time

The origins of the Spaniel family go back many centuries, and it is thought that Spain was their native homeland. Their name could be derived from 'Hispania, the Latin for Spain or the French word 'espagner', meaning 'to crouch'.

Historians believe that the Romans were responsible for bringing the Spaniel to England. By the 15th century there is written evidence, dating from the reign of Henry VI, which describes spaniels springing game for hawk and hounds.

But such was the demand for small game, such as rabbit, hare, quail, pheasant and partridge that a new method of hunting was invented to speed up the process. Spaniels were used to spring and then drive the game in the direction of fowlers, who stood ready with nets.

This method was abandoned when the gun was invented, but Spaniels still had an important role. Setting spaniels, the ancestors of today's Setters, found the game and pointed it, and Springing Spaniels flushed the game from cover, allowing it to be shot.

Spaniel breeds

Towards the end of the 18th century, the Spaniel family was beginning to be split into three specific groups, categorised by size.

First there were the Toy Spaniels, the domestic companion dogs, and then came two sporting branches: the Cockers and Field Spaniels. Cockers were used to flush out woodcock and smaller game, and were around 13kg (28lb) in weight; Field Spaniels – a blanket description to cover all working Spaniels – were taller and heavier. As shooting with the gun grew in popularity, the owners of country estates started to breed their own Spaniels which developed into distinct types. The Clumber and Sussex Spaniels are examples of this, bred specifically for their working ability and evolving into the highly recognisable breeds we know today.

The Springer got its name as this type of Spaniel became an expert at finding game and 'springing' it from the undergrowth.

In the 1800s the Duke of Norfolk started a breeding programme using larger, liver and white Spaniels.

Known as Norfolk Spaniels, they were expert at hunting and springing game, and also retrieving fallen game from land or water. These versatile hunting dogs are clearly the ancestors of the English Springer Spaniel.

Establishing the English Springer

In 1812, an English Springer enthusiast, Charles Cyril Eversfield of Denne Park, Horsham, established the Denne Park stud book which features pedigrees spanning 100 years – between 1812 and 1912.

Recorded in the earliest pedigrees are two Spaniels, Mop and Frisk, owned by Sir Thomas Fletcher Fenton Boughey. These two dogs are credited with being the foundation of the modern-day English Springer.

Facing page: Over a period of time a number of distinct Spaniel breeds, such as the Welsh Springer (pictured) were recognised.

Developing the breed

The English Springer Spaniel was officially recognised by the Kennel Club in 1902. Thae first Champion was a male called Beechgrove Will, and Fansom was the first female to gain her title. Velox Powder born in 1903, a direct descendent of Mop and Frisk after 14 generations, went on to become a Champion, winning in the field and the show ring.

Despite official recognition, there was considerable variation in type with English Springers being categorised as 23kg (50lb) and over, or under 23kg (50lb) but over 11kg (25lb). The practice of breeding litters from different Spaniel breeds, e.g. English Springer x Cocker Spaniel, was also widespread. No doubt this accounts for the range of colours recorded in the stud book in those early years which

included blue, black, liver roan, lemon and white and golden. Over the course of time, the different Spaniel breeds were allocated their own classes; Springer Spaniels were divided into the Welsh Springer Spaniel, a smaller dog with distinctive red and white colouring, and the larger English Springer Spaniel, which became became increasingly popular as both a working and companion dog. For the first half of the 20th century, the English Springer Spaniel was valued equally as a working gundog and a show dog, but after the Second World War, a split appeared in the breed, and breeders increasingly specialised in producing either working or show dogs.

The transatlantic Springer

When the Mayflower set sail for New England in 1620, there were two dogs on board: a Mastiff and a Spaniel, giving rise to the belief that Spaniels have a very long history in the USA. It appears that Springer Spaniels were highly valued for their working ability, making their mark in mixed terrain, particularly in swampland and in brambles. However, their fortunes were eclipsed as Setters took over their role, and the breed was threatened with extinction.Thanks to the endeavours of the Sporting Spaniel Society, the English Springer was reinvented using a variety of Spaniel breeds which included the Keepers Spaniel, Sussex and Clumber Spaniels, the old English

Water Spaniel, as well as the Sportsmen's Setter and Spaniel crosses. The gene bases was further widened with imports from the UK, which included Denne Lucy, from the old Velox lines. But it was Eudore Chevrier, who lived in Manitoba, Canada, who made the biggest single contribution. In just three and a half years, he imported some 250 Springers from England, and by 1925 he had over 600 English Springers in his kennels. The breed continued to thrive during the 20th century with further imports from the UK, particularly in the 1950s and 1960s. But, as in Britain, a variance of type resulted in a split between show dogs and working dogs. In addition, Springers bred in the USA developed their own look and are now quite distinct from the English type.

A dog for everyone

Today the English Springer Spaniel enjoys worldwide popularity. He is valued as a working dog, both in the field and as a sniffer dog, used by the police, armed forces, customs and excise and in prisons. He makes an impressive sight in the show ring and he is a keen competitor in dog sports. However, it is his happy, out-going disposition that is of paramount importance, making him a companion dog without parallel.

What should an English Springer look like?

The English Springer Spaniel, with his well-proportioned body, stunning coat, and melting eyes, draws admiring glances wherever he goes. So what should the perfect English Springer look like?

The aim of breeders is to produce dogs that are sound healthy, typical examples of their chosen breed, in terms of both looks and temperament. To achieve this, they are guided by a Breed Standard, which is a written blueprint describing the perfect specimen. Of course, there is no such thing as a 'perfect' dog, but breeders aspire to produce dogs that conform as closely as possible to the picture in words presented by the Breed Standard. In the show

ring, judges use the Breed Standard to assess the dogs that come before them, and it is the dog that, in their opinion, comes closest to the ideal, that will win top honours.

This has significance beyond the sport of showing, for it is the dogs that win in the ring which will be used for breeding. The winners of today are therefore responsible for passing on their genes to future generations and preserving the breed in its best form. There are some differences in the wording of the Breed Standard depending on national kennel clubs; the American Kennel Club has a far more descriptive Standard than the brief outline given in the English version and, increasingly American Springers have their own look, which distinguishes them from English-bred dogs.

General appearance

The English Springer is the raciest in build of the British land Spaniels and is highest in leg. He has a compact, well-proportioned body and is symmetrical in build.

He gives an impression of being active and merry; the American Standard states that: "His pendulous ears, soft gentle expression, sturdy build and friendly wagging tail proclaim him unmistakably a member of the ancient family of Spaniels."

Temperament

A happy, friendly disposition is a hallmark of the breed. He is eager to please, quick to learn and willing to obey. Aggressive or timid behaviour is untypical and is considered highly undesirable.

Head

It is important that the head is in proportion with the rest of the body. In terms of structure, the skull is of medium length, fairly broad and slightly rounded. As the skull rises from the foreface, it makes a stop, which is divided by a groove or fluting between the eyes. The cheeks are flat, well chiseled beneath the eyes, and the foreface is of proportionate length to the skull.

According to the American Standard: "The stop, eyebrows and chiseling of the bony structure around the eye sockets contribute to the Springer's beautiful and characteristic expression which is alert, friendly and trusting." The Springer also has well-developed nostrils, which are key to his powerful sense of smell.

Eyes

It is said that the eyes, more than any other feature, are the essence of the Springer's appeal. They are medium in size, almond-shaped, and should be neither prominent nor sunken. The typical expression is alert and kindly.

The English Standard stipulates that the required eye colour is dark hazel and that light eyes are undesirable.

The American Standard is more detailed, stating that the eye colour should harmonise with the coat colour: dark hazel in liver and white dogs, deep brown in black and white dogs.

Ears

The ears are long and wide, set in line with the eye and lying close to the cheeks. When judging the correct length, the ear leather should be long enough to reach the tip of the nose. The ears are well feathered.

Mouth

The Springer was bred to retrieve game and so he needs powerful jaws. His teeth meet in a scissor bite, meaning the teeth on the upper jaw overlap closely with the teeth on the lower jaw.

Neck

The neck is of good length and should be strong and muscular. This is important for a dog who has to hold his nose to the ground when tracking, and support his head when carrying game.

It is slightly arched at the crest blending smoothly into sloping shoulders. It should be free from throatiness.

Forequarters

The correct forequarter assembly will help to produce correct movement. The shoulders are sloping and well laid, the elbows lie close to the body and the forelegs are straight and well boned.

Body

The body is strong and compact – neither too long nor too short. The chest is deep, reaching to the level of the elbows, with a well developed forechest, but not so broad as to interfere with forward movement. The ribs are well sprung and the loin is strong and muscular, showing a slight arch.

The fine chiselling below the eyes gives an air of refinement.

Hindquarters

The rear assembly suggests strength and driving power. The thighs are broad and muscular, and the stifles and hocks are moderately bent.

Feet

The feet are rounded; they should be tight and compact with strong, thick pads.

Tail

The full tail is feathered, set on low and never carried above the level of the back. It should be lively in action.

If the tail is docked, which is legal in the USA and for working gundogs, it is carried horizontally and is in balance with the rest of the dog, showing the typical lively action. It is customarily docked to two-thirds of its full length.

Coat

The coat provides essential protection from the weather with both a topcoat and an undercoat. The topcoat is close and straight; it has a beautiful sheen and should never feel coarse. The undercoat is soft and dense. There is feathering on the ears, forelegs, body, hindquarters and tail.

Facing page: The tan markings on tricolours are highly distinctive.

Colour

The English Springer may be liver and white, black and white, or either of these colours with tan markings. The tan will be present to a lesser or greater degree on the eyebrows, lower cheeks and under the tail. The American Standard states that any amount of ticking is allowed on the body, legs and muzzle but, in reality, most American show dogs will have unblemished white colour, or the very minimum of ticking.

Movement

The English Springer's movement is highly individual; his forelegs swing straight forwards from the shoulder, throwing the feet well forward in a free and easy manner. The driving power comes from the rear, with the hindlegs reaching well under the body.

Size

The UK Standard gives an approximate height of 51 cm (20in) for both dogs and bitches. The American Standard asks for bitches to be slightly smaller, measuring 48cm (19in).

Summing up

Although the majority of English Springer Spaniels are kept as pet dogs and will never be exhibited in the show ring, it is important that breeders strive for perfection and try to produce dogs that adhere as closely as possible to the Breed Standard. This is the best way of ensuring that the English Springer remains sound in mind and body, and retains the characteristics that are unique to this very special breed.

Breeders strive to produce sound, healthy, typical English Springer Spaniels for future generations to enjoy.

What do you want from your English Springer?

There are over 200 dog breeds to choose from, so how can you be sure that the English Springer Spaniel is the right breed for you? Before you decide, you need to be 100 per cent confident that this is the breed that is best suited to your lifestyle.

Companion

Out-going, friendly and affectionate, the English Springer is, in many ways, the ideal family dog. He loves being involved in all the comings and goings of family life, and as long as mutual respect is established, he will get on well with children of all ages. It is worth bearing in mind that the English Springer is a lively, energetic dog, and will need to be controlled around toddlers. However, he is very biddable and will soon find his place in the family.

The English Springer does need extensive exercise so he may not be a good choice for those who are frail or getting on in years.

As already highlighted, an English Springer from working lines will be very different from one bred from show lines. If you are looking for a companion, you may well find that a dog from working lines is too demanding in terms of the mental stimulation he requires. A high drive dog that is tireless on the shooting field may not be ideal if you want a pet dog who is ready to chill out and fit in with family life.

Working dog

If you interested in owning a working gundog, an English Springer could well be the breed for you. Bred to find, flush out game and retrieve, the English

Springer makes good use of his amazing sense of smell, athleticism and stamina to be an outstanding worker. He responds well to instructions, always on the alert and eager to please.

Do not make the mistake of thinking a working dog will be suitable as a pet dog. An English Springer from working lines needs a job: whether this is working as a gundog, a sports competitor or as a sniffer/assistance dog, is of no matter. The fact is he needs regular mental stimulation otherwise he will become difficult to live with. This may be expressed in different ways, which can include excessive barking and whining, being destructive, or becoming anxious when left home alone.

Bearing this in mind, think twice about choosing an English Springer from working lines if you are purely looking for a pet dog.

Sports dog

The adaptable English Springer has proved his worth in all the canine sports, ranging from field trials, where he can show off his natural hunting skills, to obedience and agility where he works closely with his handler.

If you are offering a competitive home, you may find an English Springer from working lines is a good choice. There is no doubt that he will have boundless enthusiasm and energy for the task in hand. However, show-bred dogs should not be discounted as they retain the intelligence and trainability of their working cousins and may be easier to live with.

For more information, see Opportunities for English Springers.

Show dog

Do you have ambitions to exhibit your English Springer in the show ring? This is a highly competitive sport, with big entries in all the classes, so you do need the right dog to begin with. You will need to go to a breeder that specialises in show lines, and seek expert help to find a puppy with show potential.

Increasingly more emphasis is being placed on how a dog is presented in the ring, and if you exhibit an English Springer you will need to acquire the necessary grooming skills to ensure your dog looks his very best. See Caring for your English Springer.

It is also important to bear in mind that not every puppy with show potential develops into a top quality specimen, and so you must be prepared to love your English Springer and give him a home for life, even if he doesn't make the grade.

Facing page: The English Springer has the pace and athleticism for agility.

What does an English Springer want from you?

A dog cannot speak for himself, so we need to view the world from a canine perspective and work out what an English Springer needs in order to live a happy, contented and fulfilling life.

Time and commitment

First of all, an English Springer needs a commitment that you will care for him for the duration of his life, guiding him through his puppyhood, enjoying his adulthood, and being there for him in his later years. If all potential owners were prepared to make this pledge, there would be scarcely any dogs in rescue.

The English Springer Spaniel is a superb companion dog, but he does not come readymade. You need to

take charge of his education, guiding him through puppyhood and adolescence, so that he understands his place in the family. This is a clever dog and he will require a degree of mental stimulation (the amount he needs will depend on whether he is from working or show lines).

You also need to bear in mind that an English Springer needs to be a fully fledged member of the family. If he is excluded from family activities or expected to spend lengthy periods on his own, he will not only be thoroughly miserable, but he may well invent his own agenda and spend the time barking and whining or being destructive.

It is important that all dogs can cope with spending some time on their own so they don't become anxious, but the maximum time a dog should be left is four hours.

If this does not fit in with your lifestyle, you should delay owning a dog until your circumstances change.

Practical matters

The English Springer can be classed as a middle maintenance dog when it comes to looking after him. In terms of coat care, he is not as high maintenance as a long-coated breed, but he will need regular grooming to keep his coat in good order. In fact, some pet owners opt for clipping to reduce the workload.

Exercise is essential for this sporting dog – and that means in all weathers! The English Springer thrives in an active home and dog walking should be a pleasure for all concerned.

Leadership

The English Springer is not a challenging breed, but he is an active, intelligent dog who needs a leader he can respect.

It is your job to show your Springer how you want him to behave by rewarding the behaviour that you consider desirable. You need to be 100 per cent consistent, so he is left in no doubt as to what is deemed acceptable.

If he pushes the boundaries or misbehaves, interrupt his undesirable behaviour by ignoring him or refocusing his attention. As soon as he makes the 'right' decision and changes his behaviour, you can reward him handsomely.

In this way, your English Springer learns good manners without the need for force or coercion. He is living with you in peace and harmony because he respects you.

Extra
considerations

Now you have decided that an English Springer Spaniel is the dog of your dreams, you can narrow your choice so you know exactly what you are looking for.

Male or female?

The choice of male or female English Springer comes down to personal preference. Males are bigger than females, with more substance, which may be a consideration. But in terms of temperament, there is little to choose between them.

Females may be more biddable; males can become a little willful, especially when they hit adolescence. But if you persevere with kind and consistent handling, you will be rewarded hundredfold. A male Springer is a most loving and loyal companion, and

is always eager to please. A female may be prone to mood swings as a result of her seasonal cycles, but she is generally easy-going, and will be affectionate with all members of the family.

If you opt for a female, you will need to cope with her seasons, which will start at any time from nine months onwards, and occur twice yearly thereafter. During the three-week period of a season, you will need to keep your bitch away from entire males (males that have not been neutered) to eliminate the risk of an unwanted pregnancy.

Females also tend to shed their coats at this time. Many pet owners opt for neutering, which puts an end to the seasons, and also has many attendant health benefits.

The operation, known as spaying, is usually carried out at some point after the first season. The best plan is to seek advice from your vet.

An entire male may not cause many problems, although some do have a stronger tendency to mark, which could include inside the house. However, training will usually put a stop to this. An entire male will also be on the lookout for bitches in season, and this may lead to difficulties, depending on your circumstances.

Neutering (castrating) a male is a relatively simple operation, and there are associated health benefits. Again, you should seek advice from your vet.

Colour

There is a choice of four colours:

Liver and white

Black and white

Tri-colour: liver and white with tan markings

Tri-colour: black and white with tan markings

Liver and white is the most popular among pet owners and is more often seen in the show ring, although black and white Springers look very smart. Tri-colours may be harder to track down.

There are subtle differences in temperament between the sexes.

More than one?

Owning an English Springer can be addictive and you may want to expand your canine population. However, think carefully before you go ahead.

An English Springer requires training and leadership and you will need to find the time to interact with each dog individually as well as doing things together.

Be wary of a breeder who encourages you to buy two puppies from the same litter, as it is unlikely that the welfare of the puppies is their top priority.

Pups of the same or similar ages will bond with each other rather than with you – and they will get up to all sorts of mischief.

Most responsible breeders have a waiting list of potential purchasers before a litter is even born and have no need to make this type of sale. If you do decide to take on a second English Springer, wait at least 18 months so your first dog is fully trained and settled before embarking on a puppy.

In terms of gender mix, there are no hard and fast rules. English Springers get on well with each other in a male/female combination, and in single sex pairs. If you opt for a male and a female, one or both dogs will need to be neutered.

An older dog

You may decide to miss out on the puppy phase and take on an older dog instead. Such a dog may be harder to find, but sometimes a breeder may have a youngster that is not suitable for showing, but is perfect for a family pet.

In some cases, a breeder may rehome a female when her breeding career is at an end so she will enjoy the benefits of more individual attention.

It may suit your lifestyle to take on an older dog.

There are advantages to taking on an older dog, as you know exactly what you are getting. But the upheaval of changing homes can be quite upsetting, so you will need to have plenty of patience during the settling in period.

Rehoming a rescued dog

Unfortunately, a proportion of English Springer Spaniels end up in rehoming centres, often through no fault of their own.

The reasons are various, ranging from illness or death of the original owner to family breakdown, changing jobs, or the arrival of a new baby.

In some cases, the owner has made an unsuitable choice and has failed to cope with the lively, exuberant nature of an English Springer.

You may find an English Springer in all-breed rescue centre, but contacting a specialist breed club that runs a rescue scheme will probably be your best option if you decide to go down this route.

Try to find out as much as you can about a dog's history so you know exactly what you are taking on. You need to be aware of age and health status, likes and dislikes, plus any behavioural issues that may be relevant.

You need to be realistic about what you are capable of achieving so you can be sure you can give the dog in question a permanent home.

Can you give an English Springer a second chance of finding a forever home?

Regardless of the dog's previous history, you will need to give him plenty of time and be patient with him as he settles into his new home.

It may take weeks, or even months before he becomes fully integrated in the family, but if all goes well you will have the reward of knowing that you have given an English Springer a second chance.

Sourcing a puppy

Your aim is to find a healthy puppy that is typical of the breed, and has been reared with the greatest possible care. Where do you start?

A tried and trusted method of finding a puppy is to attend a dog show where your chosen breed is being exhibited. This will give you the opportunity to see lots of different English Springers of all ages, and the different colours may also be on show.

To begin with English Springers may look very much the same, but when you look closely you will detect different 'types'. They are all pure-bred English Springer Spaniels, but breeders produce dogs with a family likeness, so you can see which type you prefer.

When judging has been completed, talk to the exhibitors so you can find out more about their dogs. They may not have puppies available, but some will be planning a litter, and you may decide to put your name on a waiting list.

Internet research

The Internet is an excellent resource, but when it comes to finding a puppy, use it with care:

DO go to the website of your national kennel club.

Both the American Kennel Club (AKC) and the Kennel Club (KC) have excellent websites which will give you information about the English Springer as a breed, and what to look for when choosing a puppy. You will also find contact details for specialist breed clubs (see below).

Both sites have lists of puppies available, and you can look out for breeders of merit (AKC) and assured breeders (KC) which indicates that a code of conduct has been adhered to.

DO find details of specialist breed clubs.

On breed club websites you will find lots of useful information which will help you to care for your English Springer Spaniel. There may be contact details of breeders in your area, or you may need to go through the club secretary.

Some websites also have a list of breeders that have puppies available. The advantage of going through a breed club is that members will follow a code of ethics, and this will give you some guarantees regarding breeding stock and health checks.

If you are planning to show your English Springer you will obviously need to go to a breeder that has had some success in the ring, so you should do some additional research to discover more about their breeding lines and the type of dog they produce.

Similarly, if you want to work your English Springer in the field, you should find a breeder who has specialised in producing this type of dog.

DO NOT look at puppies for sale.

There are legitimate English Springer Spaniel

breeders with their own websites, and they may, occasionally, advertise a litter, although in most cases reputable breeders have waiting lists for their puppies.

The danger comes from unscrupulous breeders that produce puppies purely for profit, with no thought for the health of the dogs they breed from and no care given to rearing the litter.

Photos of puppies are hard to resist, but never make a decision based purely on an advertisement. You need to find out who the breeder is, and have the opportunity to visit their premises and inspect the litter before making a decision.

Questions, questions, questions

When you find a breeder with puppies available, you will have lots of questions to ask. These should include the following:

- Where have the puppies been reared? Hopefully, they will be in a home environment which gives them the best possible start in life.

- How many are in the litter?

- What is the split of males and females?

- How many have already been spoken for? The breeder will probably be keeping a puppy to show

Facing page: The breeder will need to make sure that you can provide a suitable home for an English Springer puppy.

or for breeding, and there may be others on a waiting list.

- What colours are available?

- Can I see the mother with her puppies?

- What age are the puppies?

- When will they be ready to go to their new homes?

Bear in mind puppies need to be with their mother and siblings until they are eight weeks of age otherwise they miss out on vital learning and communication skills, which will have a detrimental effect on them for the rest of their lives. You should also be prepared to answer a number of searching questions so the breeder can check if you are suitable as a potential owner of one of their precious puppies.

You will be asked some or all of the following questions:

- What is your home set up?

- Do you have children/grandchildren?

- What are their ages?

- Do you have a securely fenced garden?

- Is there somebody at home the majority of the time?

- What is your previous experience with dogs?

- Do you already have other dogs at home?

- Do you have plans to show or work your English Springer?

The breeder is not being intrusive; they just need to understand the type of home you will be able to provide in order to make the right match. Do not be offended by this; the breeder's sole aim is to find suitable, forever homes for the puppies they have produced.

Steer clear of a breeder who does not ask you questions. They may be more interested in making money out of the puppies than ensuring that they go to good homes.

They may also have taken other short-cuts which may prove disastrous, and very expensive, in terms of vet bills or plain heartache.

Health issues

In common with all pure-bred dogs, the English Springer Spaniel suffers from some hereditary problems so you need to talk to the breeder about the health status of breeding stock and find out if there are any issues of concern.

For more information, see Breed Specific Conditions.

Puppy watching

English Springer puppies are totally irresistible – you will probably find yourself wanting to take the whole litter home with you! However, you must not let your heart rule your head. Try to put your feelings to one side so that you can make an informed choice.

You need to be 100 per cent confident that the breeding stock is healthy, and the puppies have been reared with love and care, before making a commitment to buy.

Viewing a litter

It is a good idea to have a mental checklist of what to look out for when you visit a breeder. You want to see:

- A clean, hygienic environment.

- Puppies who are out-going, friendly, and eager to meet you.

- A sweet-natured mother who is ready to show off her pups.

- Puppies that are well covered, but not pot-bellied, which could be an indication of worms.

- Bright eyes, with no sign of soreness or discharge.

- Clean ears that smell fresh.

- No discharge from the ears or the nose.

- Clean rear ends – matting could indicate an upset tummy.

It is important that you see the mother with her puppies as this will give you a good idea of the temperament they are likely to inherit. It is also helpful if you can see other close relatives so you can see the type of English Springer the breeder produces.

In most cases, you will not be able to see the father (sire) as most breeders will travel some distance to find a stud dog that is not too close to their own bloodlines and complements their bitch. However, you should be able to see photos of him and be given the chance to examine his pedigree and show/working record.

Companion puppy

If you are looking for an English Springer purely as a companion, you should be guided by the breeder who will have spent hours and hours puppy watching, and will know each of the pups as an individual.

It is tempting to choose a puppy yourself, but the breeder will take into account your family set up and lifestyle and will help you pick the most suitable puppy.

Working/sports puppy

If you are planning to work your English Springer in the field or compete in one of the canine sports, you will be looking for a puppy that is keen to play and to interact with people. This will be invaluable when you train him.

There are a few basic tests you can carry out which will help you assess working potential. These tests need to be carried out on each individual puppy:

Get hold of a toy – or even a screwed up piece of paper – and throw it. A pup with a strong instinct to retrieve will run out and bring it back to you.

Drop an object, such as a saucepan lid, when the puppy's attention is focused elsewhere. He should react to the noise but recover quickly. This will indicate that he is not too sound sensitive and will tolerate gunfire.

Walk away from the pup and see if he follows. A working dog needs a degree of independence but he also needs to be people orientated.

Show puppy

If you are buying a puppy with the hope of showing him, make sure you make this clear to the breeder. A lot of planning goes into producing a litter, and although all the puppies will have been reared with equal care, there will be one or two that have show potential.

Ideally, recruit a breed expert to inspect the puppies with you so you have the benefit of their objective evaluation. The breeder will also be there to help as they will want to ensure that only the best of

What will your puppy look like as he starts to mature?

their stock is exhibited in the show ring. Wait until the puppies are between seven and eight weeks before making your choice as this gives them time to develop.

It is impossible to say with certainty that a puppy is going to be successful in the show ring; puppies go through many stages when they are growing and the ugly duckling could well surprise you. However, there are certain guidelines which are worth following:

A puppy should appear to be balanced and show correct angulation in front and behind.

The legs should be straight in front and behind; the shoulders should be sloping. The front legs should have a pronounced knee joint which is a good indication of growth potential.

Check out the tail-set – it should be low so that the tail cannot be carried above the level of the back.

The head should have the correct proportions although this is notoriously difficult to judge at this stage. Some heads start off short and chubby and lengthen with age, others are plain and narrow and broaden as the dog matures.

Puppies should have dark eyes; they may be lighter in liver and white pups. Eyes may darken with age, but bear in mind that light eyes will be faulted in the show ring.

The Breed Standard does not give guidance on markings but, generally, a classically marked show dog will have a solid coloured jacket with a white collar and legs. The head and ears will be solid colour with a white blaze rising from the muzzle to the forehead. The muzzle and the front of the neck will also be white.

Symmetrical markings are sought after in a show puppy.

An English Springer-friendly home

It may seem an age before your English Springer puppy is ready to leave the breeder and move to his new home. But you can fill the time by getting your home ready, and buying the equipment you will need. These preparations apply to a new puppy but, in reality, they are the means of creating an environment that is safe and secure for your English Springer throughout his life.

In the home

Nothing is safe when a puppy is about, and that is certainly true if you have an English Springer in the house! Everything is new and exciting for a young

puppy, and he will investigate everything with his mouth, which can lead him into all sorts of mischief. One thing is certain; a free-ranging Springer puppy cannot be trusted.

Remember, it is not only your prized possessions that are under threat – the damage a puppy can inflict on himself is equally relevant.

Trailing electric cables are a major hazard so these will need to be secured out of reach. You will need to make sure all cupboards and storage units cannot be opened or broken into.

This applies particularly in the kitchen where you may store cleaning materials, and other substances, which could be toxic to dogs. There are a number of household plants that are poisonous, so these will need to be relocated, along with breakable ornaments.

You may decide to declare upstairs off-limits and this is a sensible decision, particularly as negotiating stairs can be hazardous for a young puppy.

The best way of doing this is to install a baby gate; these can also be useful if you want to limit your English Springer's freedom in any other part of the house.

This barrier works well as your dog is separate but does not feel excluded from what is going on.

In the garden

The English Springer is a keen explorer and this could well include investigating what lies beyond your garden. For this reason, your garden will need to be securely fenced – a height of 1.5 metres (5 ft) should be a minimum requirement.

You also need to check gaps below fencing and gates, as English Springer puppies have a tendency to burrow their way out! If you have gates leading out of your property, they must have secure fastenings.

If you take a pride in your garden, you may want to think about creating an area that is free from plants and shrubs. An English Springer may share your passion for gardening but you are unlikely to appreciate his endeavours. Digging holes and uprooting plants is his idea of helping.

If you allow your English Springer free access to the garden you should be aware that there are a number of plants that are toxic to dogs, such as tulip bulbs, lily of the valley, azaleas, jasmine and daffodil flowers.

You can find a comprehensive list on the Internet. You also need to be aware that garden chemicals, such as fertilisers, fungicides and pesticides, are highly toxic so be very careful where you use them.

Swimming pools and ponds should be covered, as most puppies are fearless and, although it is easy for a puppy to take the plunge, it is virtually impossible for him to get out, potentially with lethal consequences. You will also need to designate a toileting area. This will assist the house training process, and it will also make cleaning up easier.

House rules

Before your puppy comes home, hold a family conference to make the house rules. You need to decide which rooms your puppy will have access to, and establish whether he is to be allowed on the furniture or not. It is important to start as you mean to go on. You cannot invite a puppy on to the sofa for cuddles only to decide in a few months' time that this is no longer desirable.

The English Springer likes to please, but he will push it if he doesn't know where his boundaries lie. If house rules are applied consistently, he will understand what is, and what is not, allowed, and he will learn to respect you and co-operate with you.

Buying equipment

There are some essential items of equipment you will need for your English Springer. If you choose wisely, much of it will last for many years to come.

It is worth investing in good-quality equipment.

Indoor crate

Rearing a puppy is so much easier if you invest in an indoor crate. It provides a safe haven for your puppy at night, when you have to go out during the day, and at other times when you cannot supervise him. A puppy needs a base where he feels safe and secure, and where he can rest undisturbed. An indoor crate provides the perfect den, and many adults continue to use them throughout their lives.

The crate needs to be big enough for an adult to be able to stand up, turn around, and stretch out in comfort. Ideally, it should be 15cm (6in) longer than your Springer's body and 15cm (6in) higher than his shoulder height, so you will need a crate that is sized at 91cm (36in). You will also need to consider where you are going to locate the crate. The kitchen is usually the most suitable place as this is the hub of family life. Try to find a snug corner where the puppy can rest when he wants to, but where he can also see what is going on around him, and still be with the family.

Beds and bedding

The crate will need to be lined with bedding and the best type to buy is synthetic fleece. This is warm and cosy, and as moisture soaks through it, your puppy will not have a wet bed when he is tiny and is still unable to go through the night without relieving himself. This type of bedding is machine washable and easy to dry; buy two pieces, so you have one to use while the other piece is in the wash. If you have purchased a crate, you may not feel the need to buy an extra bed, although your English Springer may like to have a bed in the family room so he feels part of household activities.

There is an amazing array of dog-beds to chose from – duvets, bean bags, cushions, baskets, igloos, mini-four posters – so you can take your pick! However, you do need to bear in mind that a puppy may enjoy chewing his bed, so it is probably worth delaying this purchase until your English Springer has finished teething.

Collar and lead

You may think that it is not worth buying a collar for the first few weeks, but the sooner your pup gets used to it, the better. A nylon lightweight collar is recommended, as most puppies will accept it without making a fuss. Be careful when you are fitting the collar that is not too tight, but equally not too loose as slipping the collar can become a favourite game...

A matching webbing lead will be fine to begin with but as your English Springer grows you will need something more substantial. Again, there are plenty to choose from; the most important consideration is that the lead has a secure trigger fastening.

An extending lead can be a useful purchase as you can give your English Springer limited freedom when it is not safe or permitted to allow him off lead. However, you should never use it when walking alongside roads; if your English Springer pulls unexpectedly, the lead may extend further than you want, with disastrous consequences.

ID

Your English Springer needs to wear some form of ID when he is out in public places. This can be in the form of a disc, engraved with your contact details, attached to the collar. When your English Springer is full-grown, you can buy an embroidered collar with your contact details, which eliminates the danger of the disc becoming detached from the collar.

It is now a legal requirement in the UK for dogs to be micro-chipped which provides a permanent form of ID. A micro-chip is the size of a grain of rice. It is injected under the skin, usually between the shoulder blades, with a special needle. It has tiny barbs on it, which dig into the tissue around where it lies, so it does not migrate from that spot.

Each chip has its own unique identification number

Facing page: You will have fun choosing toys for your English Springer!

which can only be read by a special scanner. That ID number is then registered on a national database with your name and details, so that if ever your dog is lost, he can be taken to any vet or rescue centre where he is scanned and then you are contacted. Increasingly breeders are getting puppies micro-chipped before they go to their new homes. But if this is not the case with your puppy, ask your vet to do it, maybe when he goes for his vaccinations.

Bowls

Your English Springer will need two bowls; one for food, and one for fresh drinking water, which should always be readily available. A stainless steel bowl is a good choice for food as it is tough and hygienic. Plastic bowls will almost certainly be chewed, and there is a danger that bacteria can collect in the small cracks that may appear. You can opt for a second stainless steel bowl for drinking water, or you may prefer a heavier ceramic bowl which will not be knocked over so easily.

Food

The breeder will let you know what your puppy is eating and should provide a full diet sheet to guide you through the first six months of your puppy's feeding regime – how much they are eating per meal, how many meals per day, when to increase the amounts given per meal and when to reduce the meals per day. The breeder may provide you with some food when you go and collect your puppy, but it is worth making enquiries in advance about the availability of the brand that is recommended.

Grooming gear

Your English Springer will need regular grooming to keep his coat in good order. Initially you will need:

- Soft bristle brush

- Slicker brush – check it is not too hard by dragging it cross your hand

- Metal comb – normal and fine-toothed to use on the feathering.

- Scissors – straight edged, with rounded ends.

- Nail-clippers – the guillotine type are easy to use.

- Toothbrush and toothpaste: Choose between a long-handled toothbrush or a finger brush – whichever you find easiest to use. There are flavoured canine toothpastes on the market which are acceptable to your dog.

Toys

English Springer puppies love to play, and there is no shortage of dog toys on the market. But before you get carried away with buying a vast range of toys to keep your puppy entertained, think about possible hazards.

A puppy can easily chew bits from soft or plastic toys, and if this material is ingested it can cause serious problems in the form of a blockage. This is particularly true of toys with squeakers.

The safest toys to choose are those made of hard rubber; a rubber kong which can be stuffed with food is ideal.

You can also buy tug toys, which come in a variety of materials such as faux fur, sheepskin, or even rabbit skin, but be careful how you play with your dog, particularly while he is teething.

Finding a vet

Before your puppy arrives home, you should register with a vet. Visit several vets in your local area, or speak to other pet owners that you might know, to see who they recommend.

It is so important to find a good vet – almost as much as finding a good doctor for yourself. You need to find someone with whom you can build up a good rapport and have complete faith in. Word of mouth is really the best recommendation.

When you contact a veterinary practice, find out the following:

- Does the surgery run an appointment system?

- What are the arrangements for emergency, out of hours cover?

- Do any of the vets in the practice have experience treating English Springer Spaniels?

- What facilities are available at the practice?

If you are satisfied with what you find, and the staff appear to be helpful and friendly, book an appointment so your puppy can have a health check a couple of days after you collect him.

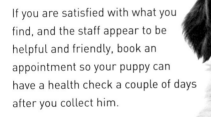

Check out a veterinary practice before your puppy arrives in his new home.

Settling in

When you first arrive home with your puppy, be careful not to overwhelm him. You and your family are hugely excited, but the puppy is in a completely strange environment with new sounds, smells and sights, which is a daunting experience, even for the boldest of pups.

Some puppies are very confident, wanting to play straightaway and quickly making friends; others need a little longer. Keep a close check on your puppy's body language and reactions so you can proceed at a pace he is comfortable with.

First, let him explore the garden. He will probably need to relieve himself after the journey home, so take him to the allocated toileting area and, when he performs, give him plenty of praise.

When you take your puppy indoors, let him investigate again. Show him his crate, and encourage him to go in by throwing in a treat. Let

him have a sniff, and allow him to go in and out as he wants to. Later on, when he is tired, you can put him in the crate while you stay in the room. In this way he will learn to settle and will not think he is being abandoned.

It is a good idea to feed your puppy in his crate, at least to begin with, as this helps to build up a positive association. It will not be long before your English Springer sees his crate as his own special den and will go there as a matter of choice. Some owners place a blanket over the crate, covering the back and sides, so that it is even more cosy and den-like.

Meeting the family

Resist the temptation of inviting friends and neighbours to come and meet the new arrival; your puppy needs to focus on getting to know his new family for the first few days. Try not to swamp your English Springer with too much attention; give him a chance to explore and find his feet. There will be plenty of time for cuddles later on!

If you have children in the family, you need to keep everything as calm as possible. Your puppy may not have met children before, and even if he has, he will still find them strange and unpredictable. A puppy can become alarmed by too much noise, or he may go to the opposite extreme and become over-excited, which can lead to mouthing and nipping.

The best plan is to get the children to sit on the floor and give them all a treat. Each child can then call the puppy, stroke him, and offer a treat. In this way the puppy is making the decisions rather than being forced into interactions he may find stressful.

If he tries to nip or mouth, make sure there is a toy at the ready, so his attention can be diverted to something he is allowed to bite. If you do this consistently, he will learn to inhibit his desire to mouth when he is interacting with people.

Right from the start, impose a rule that the children are not allowed to pick up or carry the puppy. They can cuddle him when they are sitting on the floor. This may sound a little severe, but a wriggly puppy can be dropped in an instant, sometimes with disastrous consequences.

If possible, try to make sure your English Springer is only given attention when he has all four feet on the ground. That sweet little puppy will soon become a powerful adult and you need to establish the fact that jumping up is non-productive.

Involve all family members with the day-to-day care of your puppy; this will enable the bond to develop with the whole family as opposed to just one person. Encourage the children to train and reward the puppy, teaching him to follow their commands without question.

The animal family

Care must be taken when introducing a puppy to a resident dog to ensure that relations get off on the right footing. English Springers are sociable dogs and you will rarely have problems, but it is better to be safe rather than sorry.

Your adult dog may be allowed to meet the puppy at the breeder's, which is ideal as the older dog will not feel threatened if he is away from home. But if this is not possible, allow your dog to smell the puppy's bedding (the bedding supplied by the breeder is fine) before they actually meet so he familiarises himself with the puppy's scent.

The garden is the best place for introducing the puppy, as the adult will regard it as neutral territory. He will probably take a great interest in the puppy and sniff him all over. Most puppies are naturally submissive in this situation, and your pup may lick the other dog's mouth or roll over on to his back. Try not to interfere as this is the natural way that dogs get to know each other.

You will only need to intervene if the older dog is too boisterous, and alarms the puppy. In this case, it is a good idea to put the adult on his lead so you have some measure of control.

It rarely takes long for an adult to accept a puppy, as he does not constitute a threat. This will be underlined if you make a big fuss of the older dog so that he has no reason to feel jealous. But no matter how well the two dogs are getting on, do not leave them alone unless one is crated.

Make a fuss of your resident dog so that he still feels special.

Feline friends

The English Springer has an instinct to hunt and he also has an exuberant nature. Therefore if he sees a cat on the move, he will chase. Your aim is to prevent this scenario from the onset so your English Springer learns to ignore the cat and, in time, they will establish a relationship based on mutual tolerance.

It may be easier if the cat is confined in a carrier for the first couple of meetings so your puppy has a chance to make his acquaintance in a controlled situation. Keep calling your puppy to you and rewarding him so that he does not focus too intently on the cat.

You can then graduate to holding your puppy while the cat is free, again rewarding him with a treat every time he responds to you and looks away from the cat. When you allow your puppy to go free, make sure the cat has an easy escape route, just in case he tries to chase.

This is an on-going process but, all the time your English Springer is learning that he is rewarded for ignoring the cat. In time, the novelty will wear off and the pair will mostly ignore each other. In some cases, an English and the family cat will become the best of friends and end up sharing a bed!

Feeding

The breeder will generally provide enough food for the first few days so the puppy does not have to cope with a change in diet – and possible digestive upset – along with all the stress of moving home. Some puppies eat up their food from the first meal onwards, others are more concerned by their new surroundings and are too distracted to eat. Most English Springers are pretty keen on their food so it is rare to have on-going problems. However if your puppy seems disinterested in his food, give him 10 minutes to eat what he wants and then remove the leftovers and start afresh at the next meal. Obviously if you have any concerns about your puppy in the first few days, seek advice from your vet.

It is important to give your dog space where he can eat in peace, and if you have children, you need to establish a rule that no one is to go near the dog when he is feeding. To prevent your English Springer guarding his food bowl, scatter half his rations around the bowl while he is feeding so he sees your presence in a positive light. You can also call him away from the bowl and reward him with food – maybe something extra special – which he can take from your hand. Start doing this as soon as your puppy arrives in his new home, and continue with it throughout his life.

The first night

Your puppy will have spent the first weeks of his life with either his mother or curled up with his siblings. He is then taken from everything he knows as familiar, lavished with attention by his new family, and then comes bed time when he is left all alone. It is little wonder that he feels abandoned.

The best plan is to establish a nighttime routine, and then stick to it so that your puppy knows what is expected of him. Take your puppy out into the garden to relieve himself, and then settle him in his crate. Some people leave a low light on for the puppy at night for the first week, others have tried a radio as company or a ticking clock.

A covered hot-water bottle, filled with warm water, can also be a comfort. Like people, puppies are all individuals and what works for one, does not necessarily work for another, so it is a matter of trial and error.

Be very positive when you leave your puppy on his own; do not linger, or keep returning; this will make the situation more difficult. It is inevitable that he will protest to begin with, but if you stick to your routine, he will accept that he gets left at night but you always return in the morning.

Adopt a bedtime routine so your puppy learns to settle at night.

Rescued dogs

Settling an older, rescued dog in the home is very similar to a puppy in as much as you will need to make the same preparations regarding his homecoming.

As with a puppy, an older dog will need you to be consistent, so start as you mean to go on.

There is often an initial honeymoon period when you bring a rescued dog home, where he will be on his best behaviour for the first few weeks.

It is after these first couple of weeks that the true nature of the dog will show, so be prepared for subtle changes in his behaviour.

It may be advisable to register with a reputable training club, so you can seek advice on any training or behavioural issues at an early stage.

Above all, remember that a rescued dog ceases to be a rescued dog the moment he enters his forever home and should be treated normally like any other family pet.

Facing page: A rescued dog needs time and patience as he adapts to a new home.

House training

This is an aspect of training that first-time owners dread, but if you start as you mean to go on, it will not be long before your English Springer understands what is required.

The key to successful house training is vigilance and consistency. Equally, you must be there to supervise your puppy at all times, except when he is safely tucked up in his crate. It is when a puppy is left to wander from room to room that accidents are most likely to happen.

As discussed earlier, you will have allocated a toileting area in your garden when preparing for your puppy's homecoming. You need to take your puppy to this area every time he needs to relieve himself so he builds up an association and knows why you have brought him out to the garden.

Establish a routine and make sure you take your puppy out at the following times:

- First thing in the morning
- After mealtimes
- On waking from a sleep
- Following a play session
- Last thing at night.

A puppy should be taken out to relieve himself every two hours as an absolute minimum.

If you can manage an hourly trip out, so much the better. The more often your puppy gets it right, the quicker he will learn to be clean in the house.

It helps if you use a verbal cue, such as 'Busy', when your pup is performing and, in time, this will trigger the desired response.

Do not be tempted to put your puppy out on the doorstep in the hope that he will toilet on his own. Most pups simply sit there, waiting to get back inside the house!

No matter how bad the weather is, accompany your puppy and give him lots of praise when he performs correctly.

Do not rush back inside as soon as he has finished; your puppy might start to delay in the hope of prolonging his time outside with you. Praise him, have a quick game, and then you can both return indoors.

When accidents happen

No matter how vigilant you are, there are bound to be accidents. If you witness the accident, take your puppy outside immediately, and give him lots of praise if he finishes his business out there.

If you are not there when he has an accident, do not scold him when you discover what has happened. He will not remember what he has done and will not understand why you are cross with him. Simply clean it up and resolve to be more vigilant next time.

Make sure you use a deodoriser, available in pet stores, when you clean up otherwise your pup will be drawn to the smell and may be tempted to use the same spot again.

Choosing
a diet

There are so many different types of
dog food on sale, all claiming to be the
best, so how do you know what is likely
to suit your English Springer Spaniel?

When choosing a diet, there are basically three categories to choose from:

Complete

This is probably the most popular diet as it is easy to feed and is specially formulated with all the nutrients your dog needs.

This means that you should not add any supplements or you may upset the nutritional balance. Most complete diets come in different life stages: puppy, adult maintenance and senior, so this means that your English Springer is getting what he needs when he is growing, during adulthood, and as he becomes older.

You can even get prescription diets for dogs with particular health issues.

Check protein levels provided in the diet; it is important that your English Springer has the correct level depending on his age and lifestyle.

Puppies and juniors need 25-35 per cent of protein in the diet for growth and development; 18-20 per cent protein is adequate for adult maintenance. Working dogs and lactating bitches need a higher level, around 25-28 per cent, and veterans needs a much lower level, decreasing from the basic adult maintenance diet.

There are many different brands to choose from so it is advisable to seek advice from your puppy's breeder who will have lengthy experience of feeding English Springers.

Canned/pouches

This type of food is usually fed with hard biscuit, and most English Springers find it very appetising. However, the ingredients and the nutritional value do vary significantly between the different brands so you will need to check the label.

This type of food often has a high moisture content, so you need to be sure your English Springer is getting all the nutrition he needs.

Homemade

There are some owners who like to prepare meals especially for their dogs – and it is probably much appreciated. The danger is that although the food is tasty, and your English Springer may enjoy the variety, you cannot be sure that it has the correct nutritional balance.

If this is a route you want to go down, you will need to find out the exact ratio of fats, carbohydrates, proteins, minerals and vitamins that are needed, which is quite an undertaking.

The Barf (Biologically Appropriate Raw Food) diet is another, more natural approach to feeding. Dogs are fed a diet mimicking what they would have eaten in the wild, consisting of raw meat, bone, muscle, fat, and vegetable matter. English Springers do well on this diet so it is certainly worthy of consideration. There are now a number of companies that specialise in producing the Barf diet in frozen form, which will make your job a lot easier.

Feeding regime

When your puppy arrives in his new home he will need four meals, evenly spaced throughout the day. You may decide to keep to the diet recommended by your puppy's breeder, and if your pup is thriving there is no need to change. However, if your puppy is not doing well on the food, or you have problems with supply, you will need to make a change.

When switching diets, it is very important to do it on a gradual basis, changing over from one food to the next, a little at a time, and spreading the transition over a week to 10 days. This will avoid the risk of digestive upset.

 From about 12 weeks, you can go down to three meals a day, and by six months, you can feed twice daily – a regime which should suit your English Springer for the rest of his life. There are those that advocate feeding one meal a day, but this may increase the likelihood of gastric torsion, also known as bloat.

Keep dietary changes to a minimum for the first few weeks.

This is a life threatening condition where the gut twists and fills with air. Emergency surgery is the only hope of survival. It is thought that overloading the stomach could be a potential risk, and exercising immediately before and after feeding should be avoided. To err on the side of caution, leave a minimum of one hour either side of exercise.

Food scatter

Mealtimes are the highlight of your English Springer's day – but it is all over in a matter of minutes. However, you can prolong his enjoyment – and provide mental stimulation – by allowing him to forage. Instead of giving your English Springer his food in a bowl, scatter it over a small area in the garden and give him the opportunity to find it. He will relish the opportunity to use his nose – and the result will be highly rewarding.

A food scatter is a useful device to use on days when exercise may have been limited, or simply as a means of giving your intelligent dog an occupation he will enjoy.

Faddy feeders

In common with most of the gundog breeds, the English Springer is not fussy about his food. He has a good appetite; if this changes it could be a sign that he is unwell and you may need to seek advice. However, there will always be the dog who thinks it is worth pushing his luck in the hope that you may provide superior food.

One look from those adoring eyes is enough to melt your heart, stirring you to greater efforts to find a food that he really likes. At first you may add some gravy, then you may try some chicken...The clever English Springer will quickly realise that if he holds out, tastier treats will follow.

This is a bad game to play as not only will you run out of tempting delicacies, you will also be losing your English Springer's respect. If your English Springer is turning up his nose at mealtimes, give him 10 minutes to eat what he wants, and then take up his bowl. Do not feed him treats in between meals, and give him fresh food at his next mealtime.

A food scatter gives the English Springer an opportunity to use his outstanding sense of smell.

If you continue this regime for a couple of days, your English Springer will realise that there is no percentage in holding out for better food as it never materialises.

In most cases, this is just a 'trying it on' phase, and if you cope with common sense, you will soon return to the status quo and your English Springer will be content with his normal rations.

If, however, your dog refuses all food for more than 24 hours you need to observe his behaviour to see if there are any signs of ill health, which may involve the need for a veterinary check up.

Bones and chews

Puppies love to chew, and many adult dogs also enjoy gnawing on a bone. A raw marrow bone is ideal, but make sure it is always given under supervision. White, sterilised bones do not make so much mess as a raw marrow bone, and they have the same end result of helping to keep your dog's teeth clean.

Antler chews are a popular choice with some dogs and they do seem to last a long time. Rawhide chews are best avoided; it is all too easy for an English Springer to bite off a chunk and swallow it, with the danger of it then causing a blockage.

Ideal weight

In order to help to keep your English Springer in good health it is necessary to monitor his weight. If your dog gets sufficient exercise and is fed a diet that matches his energy output, he should not put on weight. But it is something you should monitor closely. A dog that is carrying too much weight is vulnerable to many health issues; he has a reduced quality of life as he cannot exercise properly, and he will almost certainly have a reduced life expectancy.

When judging your English Springer's condition, look at him from above, and make sure you can see a definite waist. You should be able to feel his ribs, but not see them. If you are concerned about your English Springer's weight, get into the habit of visiting your veterinary surgery on a monthly basis so that you can weigh him. You can keep a record of his weight so you can make adjustments if necessary. If you are worried that your English Springer is putting on too much weight, or equally if you think he is underweight, consult your vet who will help you to plan a suitable diet.

If your English Springer is fed the correct duet, he will live a longer, healthier life.

Caring for your English Springer

The English Springer is relatively easy to care for but, like all animals, he has his own special needs which you must take on board.

Coat care

Your English Springer will need regular grooming throughout his life. It is important to start young so that he becomes accustomed to the process. Remember, a grooming session is not just about routine care, it provides an opportunity to keep a close check on your dog's overall condition.

If you spot any abnormalities – lumps, bumps, or sore places – you can seek expert advice early on, increasing the likelihood of a successful outcome.

The first step is to get your puppy used to being handled so that he accepts the attention without resentment. Initially, he will wriggle and attempt to mouth you, but just ignore his protests.

Hold him steady for a few moments, and reward him when he is still. A puppy needs to learn that it is OK to be touched all over; if you fail to do this, he may try to warn you off by growling, which could develop into more problematic behaviour.

Start by handling your puppy all over, stroking him from his head to his tail. Lift up each paw in turn, and reward him with a treat when he co-operates.

Then roll him over on to his back and tickle his tummy; this is a very vulnerable position for a dog to adopt, so do not force the issue. Be firm but gentle, and give your English Springer lots of praise when he does as you ask.

When your English Springer is happy to be handled in this way, you can introduce a soft brush and spend a few minutes working on his coat, and then reward him. He will gradually learn to accept the attention, and will relax while you groom him. A puppy will not have much feathering, but practice brushing the ears, legs, underbelly and tail so he accepts it as the norm.

The adult English Springer has a double coat – a dense undercoat and a medium length outer coat – which provide maximum protection from the weather, as well as being waterproof. The coat will need thorough brushing and combing to work through both layers. A slicker brush will be needed for the feathering, finishing off with a fine-toothed comb to eradicate tangles.

Bathing

An English Springer Spaniel should not be bathed too frequently as it has an adverse effect on the skin's natural oils. Not only does this result in a dull coat, it can also cause dry, itchy skin. However, there are times when your English Springer decides to roll in something particularly revolting, and you have no option but to bath him.

Make sure you use a mild moisturising shampoo specially formulated for dogs, and you can also use a conditioner which will improve the quality and appearance of the coat.

It is a good idea to plan your first bath while your English Springer is still small enough to handle easily. He will then become accustomed to the procedure and bath times will not become a battlefield.

Routine care

In addition to grooming, you will need to carry out some routine care.

Eyes

Check the eyes for signs of soreness or discharge. You can use a piece of cotton wool (cotton) –a separate piece for each eye – and wipe away any debris.

Ears

The ears should be clean and free from odour. You can buy specially manufactured ear wipes, or you can use a piece of cotton wool (cotton) to clean them if necessary. Do not probe into the ear canal or you risk doing more harm than good.

You will also need to trim the excess hair that grows inside the ears. Use round-ended scissors (which minimise risk of injury) and proceed with caution. Reward your English Springer for co-operating so he learns to remain still.

Teeth

Dental disease is becoming more prevalent among dogs so teeth cleaning should be seen as an essential part of your care regime. The build up of

Ears need to be checked on a regular basis and cleaned when necessary.

You can use a finger brush (pictured) or a toothbrush for teeth cleaning sessions.

The hair that grows between the pads will need to be trimmed.

Accustom your Springer to nail trimming from an early age.

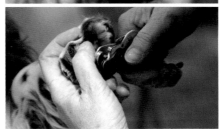

tartar on the teeth can result in tooth decay, gum infection and bad breath, and if it is allowed to accumulate, you may have no option but to get the teeth cleaned under anaesthetic.

When your English Springer is still a puppy, accustom him to teeth cleaning so it becomes a matter of routine. Dog toothpaste comes in a variety of meaty flavours, which your English Springer will like, so you can start by putting some toothpaste on your finger and gently rubbing his teeth. You can then progress to using a finger brush or a toothbrush, whichever you find most convenient.

Remember to reward your English Springer when he co-operates and then he will positively look forward to his teeth-cleaning sessions.

Feet and nails

English Springers tend to grow hair between their pads and this can become very uncomfortable if left unattended. Use your round-ended scissors and trim the hair so that it lies flat with the pad. This can be a tickly process, so be patient with your dog and reward him with some tasty treats. Nail trimming is a task dreaded by many owners, and many dogs, but if you start early on, your English Springer will get used to the task you have to perform and will not fight against it.

If you look closely you will be able to see the quick (the vein that runs through the nail), which you must avoid at all costs. If you cut the quick it will bleed profusely and cause considerable discomfort. The best policy is to trim little and often so the nails don't grow too long, and you do not risk cutting too much and catching the quick.

If you are worried about trimming your English Springer's nails, go to your vet so you can see it done properly. If you are still concerned, you can always use the services of a professional groomer.

Show presentation

If you plan to exhibit your English Springer in the show ring, you need to commit to lengthy daily grooming session in order to achieve the smooth outlines that will improve his appearance.

Presenting an English Springer to look his best requires considerable skill, and you will need to learn what is involved from an experienced exhibitor or groomer.

In addition to providing routine care, you will need to:

Hand-strip: This involves using finger and thumb to pluck out the dead hair from the coat so it lies close to the dog's body.

Show presentation:
Involves hand-stripping...

Clipping:
Electric clippers are
used to present a clean-
throated appearance and
to trim the hair on the
ears.

Thinning:
Thinning scissors will be
needed to remove excess
hair that grows on the
head to give it a smooth
contour and to remove
hair behind the ears so
they lie close to the head.

Scissoring:
Straight-edged scissors
are required to trim the
edges of the ears and to
tidy the featherings on the
legs, underbelly and tail.

Exercise

The English Springer was bred to work all day, hunting through undergrowth, clearing ditches and walls, and swimming to retrieve shot game – tasks which require a high degree of energy, stamina and endurance.

The majority of English Springers are kept as pet dogs and will not be subjected to such a rigorous regime, but an adult dog needs sufficient exercise to maintain health, fitness and wellbeing.

However, it is important not to get too carried and overdo the exercise while your Springer is growing. This is a time when bones and joints are vulnerable to injury so too much exercise, or undue stress and strain, such as climbing stairs or jumping in and out of the back of a car, should be avoided.

Initially your Springer puppy will get as much exercise as he needs playing in the garden. Once his inoculation programme has been completed he can go out on short lead-walking excursions for socialising purposes with 10 minutes' free running.

This can be stepped up gradually, month by month, until he is physically mature. Two 30-minute walks a day should be considered a minimum for an adult Springer.

This can be a mixture of lead walking and free running. The English Springer has an outstanding sense of smell so he will relish the opportunity of going to new places and investigating new surroundings.

The working English Springer was expected to retrieve from water, and you will discover that your dog is a strong and enthusiastic swimmer. If you have access to water he will enjoy playing retrieve – and you will certainly tire of it first! Before allowing your Springer to swim, make sure the water is safe with no strong currents, and check that there is an easy exit from the water. Physical exercise is important, but you also need to exercise your Springer's brain. Playing games such as retrieve and hide-and-seek is an excellent way of doing this.

The older English Springer

We are fortunate that the English Springer has a good life expectancy – generally around 12-14 years, and some may do slightly better.

As your Springer grows older, he may sleep more and he may be reluctant to go for longer walks. He may show signs of stiffness when he gets up from his bed, but these generally ease when he starts moving.

Facing page:
The English Springer
has a natural affinity
with water...

Some older Springers may have impaired vision, and some may become a little deaf, but as long as their senses do not deteriorate dramatically, this is something older dogs learn to live with If you treat your older dog with kindness and consideration, he will enjoy his later years and suffer the minimum of discomfort.

It is advisable to switch him over to a senior diet, which is more suited to his needs, and you may need to adjust the quantity, as he will not be burning up the calories as he did when he was younger and more energetic.

The older Springer will often prefer a softer diet, and you will need to keep a close check on his teeth as these may cause problems. Make sure his sleeping quarters are warm and free from draughts, and if he gets wet, make sure you dry him thoroughly.

Most important of all, be guided by your English Springer. He will have good days when he feels up to going for a walk, and other days when he would prefer to potter in the garden.

If you have a younger dog at home, this may well stimulate your Springer to take more of an interest in what is going on, but make sure he is not pestered as he needs to rest undisturbed when he is tired.

Letting go

Inevitably there comes a time when your English Springer is not enjoying a good quality of life, and you need to make the painful decision to let him go.

We would all wish that our dogs died, painlessly, in their sleep but, unfortunately, this is rarely the case.

However, we can allow our dogs to die with dignity, and to suffer as little as possible, and this should be our way of saying thank you for the wonderful companionship they have given us.

When you feel the time is drawing close, talk to your vet who will be able to make an objective assessment of your Springer's condition and will help you to make the right decision.

This is the hardest thing you will ever have to do as a dog owner, and it is only natural to grieve for your beloved Springer.

But eventually you will be able to look back on the happy memories of times spent together, and this will bring much comfort.

You may, in time, feel that your life is not complete without an English Springer, and you will feel ready to welcome a new puppy into your home.

Social skills

To live in the modern world, without fears and anxieties, your English Springer Spaniel needs to receive an education in social skills so that he learns to cope calmly and confidently in a wide variety of situations. The English Springer is a friendly, outgoing dog, with few hang-ups, and will relish the opportunity to broaden his horizons.

Early learning

The breeder will have begun a programme of socialisation by getting the puppies used to all the sights and sounds of a busy household.

You need to continue this when your pup arrives in his new home, making sure he is not worried by household equipment, such as the vacuum cleaner or the washing machine, and that he gets used to unexpected noises from the radio and television.

To begin with, your puppy needs to get used to all the members of his new family, but then you should give him the opportunity to meet friends and other people who visit your home. If you do not have children, make sure your puppy has the chance to meet and play with other people's children, making sure interactions are always supervised, so he learns that people come in small sizes too.

The English Springer is an alert dog and he will enjoy the comings and goings of a busy household. However, a young, exuberant Springer can be pushy when it comes to getting attention and he may decide that jumping up is part of his meeting and greeting strategy.

To stop this happening adopt the following training programme:

If your English Springer jumps up at you, demanding attention, simply ignore him. Turn away and do not speak to him – even to tell him off – as he will regard this as another form of attention.

Wait until he is calm and quiet, with all four feet on the ground, and then reward him by giving him the attention he craves, and maybe asking him to "sit" for a treat. You will need to be completely consistent in your training and repeat this lesson continually so that your Springer learns that his attention-seeking strategies do not work. He will only get attention when you are ready to give it.

If visitors come to the house, keep your Springer on a lead and make sure he is sitting before the visitor gives him attention. As your Springer learns to control his behaviour you can ask the visitor to give him a treat when he has all four feet on the ground.

Separation Anxiety

The English Springer loves his family; his preferred choice is always to be with his people rather than spending time on his own. For this reason, it is important to teach your Springer that he can cope on his own, otherwise he will become increasingly anxious and may develop behavioral problems, such as excessive barking, whining or becoming destructive when he is left home alone.

You can take the stress out of separations in the following ways:

Use an indoor crate overnight and at times when you are away from home. Your Springer will learn to settle in his 'den', and if he does not have a chance to roam, he cannot get up to mischief.

Keep your comings and goings low-key so your Springer does not back-chain events, becoming worried when he anticipates your departures, and over-excited when he senses your return.

Provide a boredom busting toy, such a kong, and fill it with food. This will give your Springer an occupation while you are away.

Build up the length of separations gradually, so your Springer learns there is no need to be anxious as you always come back.

The outside world

When your puppy has completed his vaccinations, he is ready to venture into the outside world. English Springers are generally pretty confident but there is a lot for a youngster to take on board, so do not swamp him with too many new experiences when you first set out. Obviously you need to work at lead-training before you go on your first expedition.

There will be plenty of distractions to deal with, so you do not want the additional problem of coping with a dog that is pulling or lagging on the lead Hopefully, you can set off with your Springer walking by your side on a loose lead.

He may need additional encouragement when you venture further afield, so arm yourself with some extra special treats, which will give him a good reason to focus on you when required!

Progress at a pace that suits your own, individual puppy.

Start socialising your puppy in a quiet area with light traffic, and only progress to a busier place when he is ready. There is so much to see and hear – people (maybe carrying bags or umbrellas), pushchairs, bicycles, cars, lorries, machinery – so give your puppy a chance to take it all in. If he does appear worried, do not fall into the trap of sympathising with him or over-doing the reassurance. This will only teach your pup that he had a good reason to be concerned and, with luck, you will rescue him if he feels scared.

Instead, give him a little space so he does not have to confront whatever he is frightened of, and distract him with a few treats. Then encourage him to walk past, using an encouraging tone of voice, never forcing him by yanking on the lead. Reward him for any forward movement, and your puppy will soon learn that he can trust you, and there is nothing to fear. Your pup also needs to continue his education in canine manners, started by his mother and by his littermates, as he needs to be able to greet all dogs calmly, giving the signals that say he is friendly and offers no threat. If you have a friend who has a dog of sound temperament, this is an ideal way to get your puppy used to social interactions. As he gets older and more established, you can widen his circle of canine acquaintances.

Training classes

A training class will give your English Springer the opportunity to work alongside other dogs in a controlled situation, and he will also learn to focus on you in a different, distracting environment. Both these lessons will be vital as your dog matures. However, the training class needs to be of the highest calibre or you risk doing more harm than good. Before you go along with your puppy, attend a class as an observer to make sure you are happy with what goes on.Find out the following:

- How much training experience do the instructors have?

- Are the classes divided into appropriate age categories?

- Do the instructors have experience training English Springers?

- Do they use positive, reward-based training methods?

If the training class is well run, it is certainly worth attending. Both you and your Springer will learn useful training exercises; it will increase his social skills, and you will have the chance to talk to lots of like-minded dog enthusiasts.

Training guidelines

The English Springer is a highly intelligent dog and he relishes the opportunity to use his brain and to interact with members of his human family. Training, even at a basic level, is essential as a Springer will become bored and hard to manage if he is deprived of mental stimulation and is uncertain of his status in the family pack.

You will be keen to get started but in your rush to get training underway, do not neglect the fundamentals which could make the difference between success and failure.

You need to get into the mindset of an English Springer working out what motivates him and, equally, what makes him switch off.

Decide on your priorities for training, and then think of ways of making your training as much fun – and as positive – as possible.

When you start training, try to observe the following guidelines:

Choose an area that is free from distractions so your puppy will focus on you. You can move on to a more challenging environment as your pup progresses.

Do not train your puppy just after he has eaten or when you have returned from exercise. He will either be too full, or too tired, to concentrate.

Do not train if you are in a bad mood, or if you are short of time. These sessions always end in disaster!

Providing a worthwhile reward is an essential tool in training. The English Springer will work for a toy and for treats so you can employ a flexible approach depending on what you are teaching.

If you decide to use a toy, make sure it is only brought out for training sessions so that it accrues added value.Keep your verbal cues simple, and always use the same one for each exercise.

For example, when you ask your puppy to go into the down position, the cue is "down", not "lie down, "get down", or anything else.

Remember, your Springer does not speak English; he associates the sound of the word with the action. If your dog is finding an exercise difficult, break it down into small steps so it is easier to understand.

Do not make your training sessions boring and repetitious; your English Springer will lose concentration and will cease to co-operate.

Do not train for too long, particularly with a young puppy, who has a very short attention span, and always end training sessions on a positive note. This does not necessarily mean getting an exercise right.

If your pup is tired and making mistakes, ask him to do a simple exercise so you have the opportunity to praise and reward him.

You may well find that he benefits from having a break and will make better progress next time you try. Above all, make training fun so you and your Springer enjoy spending quality time together.

First lessons

Like all puppies, a young English Springer will soak up new experiences like a sponge, so training should start from the time your pup arrives in his new home.

Wearing a collar

You may, or may not, want your Springer to wear a collar all the time. But when he goes out in public places he will need to be on a lead, and so he should be used to the feel of a collar around his neck. The best plan is to accustom your pup to wearing a soft collar for a few minutes at a time until he gets used to it.

Fit the collar so that you can get at least two fingers between the collar and his neck. Then have a game to distract his attention. This will work for a few moments; then he will stop, put his back leg up behind his neck and scratch away at the peculiar itchy thing which feels so odd.

Bend down, rotate the collar, pat him on the head

and distract him by playing with a toy or giving him a treat. Once he has worn the collar for a few minutes each day, he will soon ignore it and become used to it. Remember, never leave the collar on the puppy unsupervised, especially when he is outside in the garden, or when he is in his crate, as it could get snagged, causing serious injury.

Walking on the lead

This is a simple exercise but the English Springer can get impatient and decide that pulling on the lead is better than walking by your side. It is therefore a good idea to master the basics, and for your Springer to learn good lead walking manners before problems with pulling arise.

Once your puppy is used to the collar, take him outside into your secure garden where there are no distractions.

Attach the lead and, to begin with, allow him to wander with the lead trailing, making sure it does not become snagged on anything. Then pick up the lead and follow the pup where he wants to go; he needs to get used to the sensation of being attached to you.

The next stage is to get your Springer to follow you, and for this you will need some treats. To give

Facing page: The aim is for your English Springer to walk on a loose lead, regardless of distractions.

yourself the best chance of success, make sure the treats are high value – cheese, sausage or cooked liver – so your puppy is motivated to work with you.

Show him you have a treat in your hand, and then encourage him to follow you. Walk a few paces, and if he is walking with you, stop and reward him. If he puts on the brakes, simply change direction and lure him with the treat.

Next, introduce some changes of direction so your puppy is walking confidently alongside you. At this stage, introduce a verbal cue – "heel" – when your puppy is in the correct position. You can then graduate to walking your puppy outside the home, as long as he has completed his vaccination programme, starting in quiet areas and building up to busier environments.

Training strategy

Despite your best efforts, you may find yourself trying to cope with a dog that pulls on the lead. This soon becomes an unpleasant experience, so it is important to adopt a strategy that makes him realise there is no percentage in pursuing this policy.

Restrict lead training to the garden in the initial stages so you are working in an environment that is free from distractions.

Walk a few paces, being very aware of any tension on the lead. If you feel the lead tighten and your Springer is attempting to get ahead of you, stop, change direction, and set off again.

Your Springer needs to understand that pulling ahead has exactly the opposite effect to the one he wants. Rather than calling the tune, he has to co-operate with you.

Keep a good supply of tasty treats and remember only reward – with food and with verbal praise – when he is walking on a loose lead by your side.

The mistake made by many owners at this stage is to use the treats to lure the dog into position rather than rewarding him for the correct behaviour.

Keep training sessions short, and when you are ready to venture into the outside world, do not be too ambitious to begin with.

Build up the level of distraction and the duration of lead walking only when your Springer is consistently showing the behaviour you want.

Come when called

The English Springer is fundamentally an obedient dog that likes to please. However, there are times when he gets distracted. There are so many enticing smells, places to explore, people and dogs to meet... He will never stray too far away, but he may get into the habit of coming in his own time unless you make the recall a rewarding exercise.

Your aim must be to make coming when called even more rewarding than whatever is on your Springer's personal agenda.

This needs to be built up over a period of time, with lots of repetition so your Springer sees you as someone that is always ready to reward him, rather than as an irate owner who is trying to spoil his fun.

Hopefully, the breeder will have laid the foundations simply by calling the puppies to "come" when it is dinnertime, or when they are moving from one place to another.

You can build on this when your puppy arrives in his new home, calling him to "come" when he is in a confined space, such as the kitchen. This is a good place to build up a positive association with the verbal cue – particularly if you ask your puppy to "come" to get his dinner!

The next stage is to transfer the lesson to the garden. Arm yourself with some treats, and wait until your puppy is distracted. Then call him, using a higher-pitched, excited tone of voice.

At this stage, a puppy wants to be with you, so capitalise on this and keep practising the verbal cue, and rewarding your puppy with a treat and lots of praise when he comes to you.

Now you are ready to introduce some distractions. Try calling him when someone else is in the garden, or wait a few minutes until he is investigating a really interesting scent. When he responds, make a really big fuss of him and give him extra treats so he knows it is worth his while to come to you.

If your puppy responds, immediately reward him with a treat. If he is slow to come, run away a few steps and then call again, making yourself sound really exciting. Jump up and down, open your arms wide to welcome him; it doesn't matter how silly you look, he needs to see you as the most fun person in the world.

When you have a reliable recall in the garden, you can venture into the outside world. Do not be too ambitious to begin with; try a recall in a quiet place with the minimum of distractions so you can be more certain of success.

Do not make the mistake of only asking your dog to come at the end of his allotted exercise period. What is the incentive in coming back to you if all you do is clip on his lead, marking the end of his free time?

Instead, call your dog at random times, giving him a treat and a stroke, and then letting him go free again. In this way, coming to you – and focusing on you – is always rewarding.

Stationary exercises

The Sit and Down are easy to teach, and mastering these exercises will be rewarding for both you and your English Springer. This is a breed that can be boisterous, particularly during adolescence, so it is useful if you have a means of bringing proceedings to a standstill before everyone gets carried away!

Sit

The best method is to lure your English Springer into position, and for this you can use a treat or his food bowl.

Hold the reward (a treat or food bowl) above his head. As he looks up, he will lower his hindquarters and go into a sit.

Practise this a few times and when your puppy

understands what you are asking, introduce the verbal cue, "sit".

When your Springer understands the exercise, he will respond to the verbal cue alone, and you will not need to reward him every time he sits. However, it is a good idea to give him a treat on a random basis when he co-operates to keep him guessing!

Down

This is an important lesson, and can be a lifesaver if an emergency arises and you need to bring your English Springer to an instant halt.

You can start with your dog in a sit or a stand for this exercise. Stand or kneel in front of him and show him you have a treat in your hand. Hold the treat just in front of his nose and slowly lower it towards the ground, between his front legs.

As your Springer follows the treat he will go down on his front legs and, in a few moments, his hindquarters will follow. Close your hand over the treat so he doesn't cheat and get the treat before he is in the correct position. As soon as he is in the down, give him the treat and lots of praise.

Keep practising, and when your Springer understands what you want, introduce the verbal cue, "down".

Facing page: Teaching a dog the 'down' exercise introduces an important measure of control.

Control exercises

These exercises are not the most exciting, but they are important in establishing a relationship of mutual respect with your English Springer.

Wait

This exercise teaches your Springer to wait in position until you give the next command; it differs from the stay exercise where he must stay where you have left him for a more prolonged period.

The most useful application of wait is when you are getting your dog out of the car and you need him to stay in position until you clip on his lead.

Start with your puppy on the lead to give you a greater chance of success. Ask him to sit, and stand in front him.

Step back one pace, holding your hand, palm flat, facing him. Wait a second and then come back to

stand in front of him. You can then reward him and release him with a word, such as "OK".

Practise this a few times, waiting a little longer before you reward him, and then introduce the verbal cue, "wait".

You can reinforce the lesson by using it in different situations, such as asking your Springer to "wait" before you put his food bowl down.

Stay

You need to differentiate this exercise from the wait by using a different verbal cue.

Start with your Springer in the down as he is most likely to be secure in this position. Stand by his side and then step forwards, with your hand held back, palm facing the dog.

Step back, release him, and then reward him. Practise until your Springer understands the exercise and then introduce the verbal cue, "stay".

Gradually increase the distance you can leave your puppy, and increase the challenge by walking around him – and even stepping over him – so that he learns he must stay until you release him.

Leave

A response to this verbal cue means that your English Springer will learn to give up a toy on request, and it follows on that he will give up anything when he is asked, which is very useful if he has got hold of a forbidden object.

The leave command can be taught quite easily when you are first playing with your puppy. As you gently take a toy from his mouth, introduce the verbal cue, "leave", and then praise him. If he is reluctant, swap the toy for another toy or a treat. This will usually do the trick.

Do not try to pull the toy from his mouth if he refuses to give it up, as you will make the situation confrontational.

The best strategy is to let the toy go dead in your hand, and then swap it for a new toy, or a really high-value treat, so this becomes the better option.

Remember to make a big fuss of your Springer when he does as you ask. Being in your good books means a lot to him so never stint on giving him verbal praise and telling him he is the best dog in the world!

Opportunities for English Springers

The English Springer has a strong work ethic and he thrives on being given things to do. He is prepared to take on any new challenge, and with positive, reward-based training, he will make his mark in any sport you care to try.

Good Citizen Scheme

The Kennel Club Good Citizen Scheme was introduced to promote responsible dog ownership, and to teach dogs basic good manners. In the US there is one test; in the UK there are four award levels: Puppy Foundation, Bronze, Silver and Gold.

Exercises within the scheme include:

- Walking on lead

- Road walking

- Control at door/gate.

- Food manners

- Recall

- Stay

- Send to bed

- Emergency stop

Obedience

If your English Springer has mastered basic obedience, you may want to get involved in competitive obedience. The exercises include: heelwork at varying paces with dog and handler following a pattern decided by the judge, stays, recalls, retrieves, sendaways, scent discrimination and distance control. The exercises get progressively harder as you progress up the classes. An English Springer will have no trouble learning these exercise but you need to be aware that this discipline calls for a very high degree of precision and accuracy which does not suit all dogs, or all handlers.

Rally O

If you do not want to get involved in the rigours of Competitive Obedience, you may find that a sport called Rally O is more to your liking. This is loosely based on Obedience, and also has a few exercises borrowed from Agility when you get to the highest levels. Handler and dog must complete a course, in the designated order, which has a variety of different exercises which could number from 12 to 20.

The course is timed and the team must complete within the time limit that is set, but there are no bonus marks for speed. The great advantage of Rally O is that it is very relaxed, and anyone can compete; indeed, it has proved very popular for handlers with disabilities as they are able to work their dogs to a high standard and compete on equal terms with other competitors.

Agility

This is a demanding sport, a perfect match for the English Springer, with his quick mind and athletic physique. In Agility, the dog completes an obstacle course, which includes jumps, tunnels, weaving poles and contact equipment (A-frame, dog-walk and seesaw), under the guidance of his owner.

The classes are categorised by height, and jumps will go up or down accordingly. In competition, each dog completes the course individually and is assessed on both time and accuracy.

The dog that completes the course with the fewest faults, in the fastest time, wins the class.

Flyball

This is a fast and furious sport, which is always accompanied by a huge amount of enthusiastic barking. It is a team sport where four dogs are selected to run in a relay race against an opposing team.

The dogs are sent out by their handlers to jump four hurdles, catch the ball from the flyball box and then return over the hurdles.

The teams compete against the clock, and a heat is decided when the fourth dog crosses the finishing line. The English Springer is a natural retriever, and if this instinct is encouraged early on with lots of play and reward, he will soon become ball obsessed, which is the key to a great flyball dog.

Field trials

These are highly competitive, sometimes arduous events, which are staged to replicate a day's shooting in the field. A well-trained English Springer Spaniel from working lines can excel in these competitions, showcasing their ability to carry out the skills they were bred for.

Dogs are asked to retrieve shot game from any type of terrain including, swamp, thick undergrowth and water.

Facing page: The English Springer is highly prized on the hunting field.

They are also assessed on blind retrieves, where they are sent out to retrieve shot game when they haven't seen it fall.

If field trials sound a little ambitious, you may prefer rough shooting where your dog uses his natural working skills, but without the pressure of competition.

Tracking

The English Springer has an excellent nose and is a natural choice for this demanding sport where the dog must learn to follow scent trails of varying age, over different types of terrain.

In the UK tracking is incorporated into Working Trials where a dog must compete in two other elements (control and agility) but in the US it is a sport in its own right.

Showing

Exhibiting a dog in the show ring sounds easy but, in fact, it entails a lot of training and preparation.

Your English Springer will have to be calm and confident in the busy show atmosphere, so you need to work on his socialization, and also on your grooming skills so you present him to perfection.

You will also need to take him to ringcraft classes so

you both learn what is required in the ring.

Your Springer will be subjected to a detailed 'hands on' examination by the judge; he must learn to stand still in a show pose and to move on a loose lead so the judge can assess his gait.

Showing at the top level is highly addictive, so watch out, once you start, you will never have a free date in your diary!

Dancing with dogs

This is a relatively new discipline and is growing in popularity, despite the hard work that is involved.

Dog and handler perform a choreographed routine to music, allowing the dog to show off an array of tricks and moves, which delight the crowd.

There are two categories: heelwork to music where heel work in different positions make up the larger percentage of the routine, and canine freestyle which allow the dog to work at a greater distance from the handler, and will include some of the more spectacular moves.

Both categories demand a huge amount of training but if you keep sessions light-hearted, with plenty of tasty food rewards on offer, the English Springer will prove to be a real crowd-pleaser!

Health care

We are fortunate that the English Springer Spaniel is a healthy breed and with good routine care, a well-balanced diet, and sufficient exercise, most will experience few health problems.

However, it is your responsibility to put a programme of preventative health care in place, and this should start from the moment your puppy, or older dog, arrives in his new home.

Vaccinations

Dogs are subject to a number of contagious diseases. In the old days, these were killers, and resulted in heartbreak for many owners.

Vaccinations have now been developed, and the occurrence of the major infectious diseases is now very rare. However, this will only remain the case if all pet owners follow a strict policy of vaccinating their dogs. There are vaccinations available for the following diseases:

Adenovirus (Canine Adenovirus): This attacks the liver and affected dogs have a classic 'blue eye'.

Distemper: A viral disease which causes chest and gastro-intestinal damage. The brain may also be affected, leading to fits and paralysis.

Parvovirus: Causes severe gastro enteritis, and most commonly affects puppies.

Leptospirosis: This bacterial disease is carried by rats and affects many mammals, including humans. It causes liver and kidney damage.

Rabies: A virus that affects the nervous system and is invariably fatal. The first signs are abnormal behaviour when the infected dog may bite another animal or a person. Paralysis and death follow. Vaccination is compulsory in most countries. In the UK, dogs travelling overseas must be vaccinated.

Kennel cough: There are several strains of kennel cough, but they all result in a harsh, dry, cough. This disease is rarely fatal; in fact most dogs make a good recovery within a matter of weeks and show few signs of ill health while they are affected.

However, kennel cough is highly infectious among dogs that live together so, for this reason, most boarding kennels will insist that your dog is protected by the vaccine, which is given as nose drops.

Lyme disease: This is a bacterial disease transmitted by ticks. The first signs are limping, but the heart, kidneys and nervous system can also be affected. The ticks that transmit the disease occur in specific regions, such as the north-east states of the USA, some of the southern states, California and the upper Mississippi region.

Lyme disease is still rare in the UK so vaccinations are not routinely offered.

Vaccination programme

In the USA, the American Animal Hospital Association advises vaccination for core diseases, which they list as distemper, adenovirus, parvovirus and rabies. The requirement for vaccinating for non-core diseases – leptospirosis, lyme disease and kennel cough – should be assessed depending on a dog's individual risk and his likely exposure to the disease. In the UK, vaccinations are routinely given for distemper, adenovirus, leptospirosis and parvovirus.

In most cases, a puppy will start his vaccinations at around eight weeks of age, with the second part given a fortnight later. However, this does vary depending on the individual policy of veterinary practices, and the incidence of disease in your area. You should also talk to your vet about whether to give annual booster vaccinations. This depends on an individual dog's levels of immunity, and how long a particular vaccine remains effective.

Parasites

No matter how well you look after your English Springer you will have to accept that parasites (internal and external) are ever present, and you need to take preventative action.

Internal parasites: As the name suggests, these parasites live inside your dog. Most will find a home in the digestive tract, but there is also a parasite that lives in the heart. If infestation is unchecked, a dog's health will be severely jeopardised, but routine preventative treatment is simple and effective.

External parasites: These parasites live on your dog's body – in his skin and fur, and sometimes in his ears.

Roundworm

This is found in the small intestine, and signs of infestation will be a poor coat, a pot belly, diarrhoea and lethargy. Pregnant mothers should be treated, but it is almost inevitable that parasites will be passed on to the puppies. For this reason, a breeder will start a worming programme, which you will need to continue. Ask your vet for advice on treatment, which will be ongoing throughout your dog's life.

Tapeworm

Infection occurs when fleas and lice are ingested; the adult worm takes up residence in the small intestine, releasing mobile segments (which contain eggs) that can be seen in a dog's faeces as small rice-like grains.

The only other obvious sign of infestation is irritation

of the anus. Again, routine preventative treatment is required throughout your Springer's life.

Heartworm

This parasite is transmitted by mosquitoes, and so will only occur where these insects thrive. A warm environment is needed for the parasite to develop, so it is more likely to be present in areas with a warm, humid climate. However, it is found in all parts of the USA, although its prevalence does vary. At present, heartworm is rarely seen in the UK. Heartworm live in the right side of the heart. Larvae can grow up to 14 inches (35.5cm) in length. A dog with heartworm is at severe risk from heart failure, so preventative treatment, as advised by your vet, is essential. Dogs living in the USA should have regular blood tests to check for the presence of infection.

Lungworm

Lungworm, or *Angiostrongylus vasorum*, is a parasite that lives in the heart and major blood vessels supplying the lungs. It can cause many problems, such as breathing difficulties, blood-clotting problems, sickness and diarrhoea, seizures, and can be fatal. The parasite is carried by slugs and snails, and the dog becomes infected when ingesting these, often accidentally when rummaging through undergrowth. Lungworm is not common, but it is on the increase and a responsible owner should be aware of it. Fortunately, it is easily preventable and even affected dogs usually make a full recovery if treated early enough. Your vet will be able to advise you on the risks in your area and what form of treatment may be required.

Fleas

A dog may carry dog fleas, cat fleas, and even human fleas. The flea stays on the dog only long enough to have a blood meal and to breed, but its presence will result in itching and scratching. If your dog has an allergy to fleas, which is usually a reaction to the flea's saliva, he will scratch himself until he is raw.

Preventative treatment needs be administered on a routine basis; this can be in the form of a tablet, spot-on treatment, an insecticidal spray or shampoo.

Ask your vet for advice on what product to use.. Bear in mind that the whole environment your dog lives in will need to be sprayed, and all other pets living in your home will also need to be treated.

How to detect fleas

You may suspect your dog has fleas, but how can you be sure? There are two methods to try.

Run a fine comb through your dog's coat, and see if you can detect the presence of fleas on the skin, or clinging to the comb. Alternatively, sit your dog on white paper and rub his back. This will dislodge faeces from the fleas, which will be visible as small brown specks. To double check, shake the specks on to some damp cotton wool (cotton). Flea faeces consists of the dried blood taken from the host, so if the specks turn a lighter shade of red, you know your dog has fleas.

Ticks

These are blood-sucking parasites which are most frequently found in rural areas where sheep or deer are present. The main danger is their ability to pass Lyme disease to both dogs and humans. Lyme disease is prevalent in some areas of the USA, although it is still rare in the UK.

The treatment you give your dog for fleas generally works for ticks, but you should discuss the best product to use with your vet.

How to remove a tick

If you spot a tick on your dog, do not try to pluck it off as you risk leaving the hard mouth parts embedded in his skin. The best way to remove a tick is to use a fine pair of tweezers or you can buy a tick remover.

Grasp the tick head firmly and then pull the tick straight out from the skin. If you are using a tick remover, check the instructions, as some recommend a circular twist when pulling. When you have removed the tick, clean the area with mild soap and water.

Ear mites

These parasites live in the outer ear canal. The signs of infestation are a brown, waxy discharge, and your dog will continually shake his head and scratch his ear.

If you suspect your Springer has ear mites, a visit to the vet will be needed so that medicated ear drops can be prescribed.

Fur mites

These small, white parasites are visible to the naked eye and are often referred to as 'walking dandruff'. They cause a scurfy coat and mild itchiness. However, they are zoonetic – transferable to humans – so prompt treatment with an insecticide prescribed by your vet is essential.

Harvest mites

These are picked up from the undergrowth, and can be seen as a bright orange patch on the webbing between the toes, although this can be found elsewhere on the body, such as on the ear flaps. Treatment is effective with the appropriate insecticide.

Skin mites

There are two types of parasite that burrow into a dog's skin. *Demodex canis* is transferred from a mother to her pups while they are feeding. Treatment is with a topical preparation, and sometimes antibiotics are needed.

The other skin mite, *Sarcoptes scabiei*, causes intense itching and hair loss. It is highly contagious, so all dogs in a household will need to be treated, which involves repeated bathing with a medicated shampoo.

Common ailments

As with all living animals, dogs can be affected by a variety of ailments. Most can be treated effectively after consulting with your vet, who will prescribe appropriate medication and will advise you on how to care for your dog's needs.

Here are some of the more common problems that could affect your English Springer Spaniel with advice on how to deal with them.

Anal glands

These are two small sacs on either side of the anus, which produce a dark-brown secretion that dogs use when they mark their territory. The anal glands should empty every time a dog defecates but if they become blocked or impacted, a dog will experience increasing discomfort. He may nibble at his rear end,

or scoot his bottom along the ground to relieve the irritation. Treatment involves a trip to the vet, who will empty the glands manually. It is important to do this without delay or infection may occur.

Dental problems

Good dental hygiene will do much to minimise gum infection and tooth decay, which is why teeth cleaning should be part of your regular care routine. If tartar accumulates to the extent that you cannot remove it by brushing, the vet will need to intervene. In a situation such as this, an anaesthetic will need to be administered so the tartar can be removed manually.

Diarrhoea

There are many reasons why a dog has diarrhoea, but most commonly it is the result of scavenging, a sudden change of diet, or an adverse reaction to a particular type of food.

If your dog is suffering from diarrhoea, the first step is to withdraw food for a day. It is important that he does not dehydrate, so make sure that fresh drinking water is available. However, drinking too much can increase the diarrhoea, which may be accompanied by vomiting, so limit how much he drinks at any one time. After allowing the stomach to rest, feed a bland diet, such as white fish or chicken with boiled rice, for a few days. In most cases, your dog's motions will return to normal and you can resume usual feeding, although this should be done gradually.

However, if this fails to work and the diarrhoea persists for more than a few days, you should consult you vet. Your dog may have an infection which needs to be treated with antibiotics, or the diarrhoea may indicate some other problem which needs expert diagnosis.

Ear infections

The English Springer has drop ears which means that air does not circulate freely, potentially creating an ideal environment for infection. A healthy ear is clean with no sign of redness or inflammation, and no evidence of a waxy brown discharge or a foul odour. If you see your dog scratching his ear, shaking his head, or holding one ear at an odd angle, you will need to consult your vet.

The most likely causes are ear mites, an infection, or there may be a foreign body, such as a grass seed, trapped in the ear. Depending on the cause, treatment is with medicated ear drops, possibly containing antibiotics. If a foreign body is suspected, the vet will need to carry out further investigations.

Eye problems

The English Springer has medium-sized eyes, which are neither sunken nor prominent. This lack of exaggeration means that a Springer's eyes should not be predisposed to infection or vulnerable to injury or trauma, which is the case with breeds such as the Pekingese, which have somewhat bulging eyes.

However, if your Springer's eyes look red and sore, he may be suffering from conjunctivitis. This may, or may not be accompanied with a watery or a crusty discharge. Conjunctivitis can be caused by a bacterial or viral infection, it could be the result of an injury, or it could be an adverse reaction to pollen.

You will need to consult your vet for a correct diagnosis, but in the case of an infection, treatment with medicated eye drops is effective.

Foreign bodies

In the home, puppies – and some older dogs – cannot resist chewing anything that looks interesting. The toys you choose for your dog should be suitably robust to withstand damage, but children's toys can be irresistible. Some dogs will chew – and swallow – anything from socks, tights, and any other items from the laundry basket to golf balls and stones from the garden. Obviously, these items are indigestible and could cause an obstruction in your dog's intestine, which is potentially lethal.

The signs to look for are vomiting, and a tucked up posture. The dog will often be restless and will look as though he is in pain. In this situation, you must get your dog to the vet without delay, as surgery may be needed to remove the obstruction.

Heatstroke

As a working gundog, the English Springer has no tendency towards exaggeration in his physical conformation. Therefore, he is not prone to over-heating as is the case with breeds, such as the Bulldog or the Boxer, that have short muzzles and up-turned noses.

However, all dogs can be affected by heatstroke – and temperatures do not need to be extreme for this to occur.

If the weather is warm, make sure your Springer has access to shady areas, and wait for a cooler part of the day before going for a walk.

Be extra careful if you leave your Springer in the car as the temperature can rise dramatically – even on a cloudy day. Heatstroke can happen very rapidly, and unless you are able to lower your dog's temperature, it can be fatal.

If your dog appears to be suffering from heatstroke, lie him flat and work at lowering his temperature by spraying him with cool water and covering him with wet towels.

As soon as he has made some recovery, take him to the vet, where cold intravenous fluids can be administered.

Lameness/limping

There are a wide variety of reasons why a dog can go lame, from a simple muscle strain, to a fracture, ligament damage, or more complex problems with the joints. If you are concerned about your dog, do not delay in seeking help.

As your Springer becomes more elderly, he may suffer from arthritis, which you will see as general stiffness, particularly when he gets up after resting. It will help if you ensure his bed is in a warm draught-free location, and if he gets wet after exercise, you must dry him thoroughly. If he seems to be in pain, consult your vet who will be able to help with pain relief medication.

Skin problems

If your dog is scratching or nibbling at his skin, first check he is free from fleas. There are other external parasites which cause itching and hair loss, but you will need a vet to help you find the culprit.

An allergic reaction is another major cause of skin problems. It can be quite an undertaking to find the cause of the allergy, and you will need to follow your vet's advice, which often requires eliminating specific ingredients from the diet, as well as looking at environmental factors.

Breed-specific disorders

Like all pedigree dogs, the English Springer does have some breed-related disorders. If diagnosed with any of the diseases listed here, it is important to remember that they can affect offspring so breeding from such dogs should be discouraged.

There are now recognised screening tests to enable breeders to check for affected individuals and hence reduce the prevalence of these diseases within the breed.

DNA testing is also becoming more widely available, and as research into the different genetic diseases progresses, more DNA tests are being developed.

Epilepsy

There appears to be an inherited pattern to epilepsy, a condition where dogs suffer fits or seizures. The age of onset varies, as does the severity. Dogs may have occasional fits, or they may come n clusters and occur frequently.

Medication is effective in controlling fits, but there is no cure. An affected dog will need to be on medication for the rest of his life, and should not be used for breeding.

Eye disorders

Cataract

Cataracts are an opacification of the lens that tends to occur in older dogs. There are varying degrees of severity, with the inherited form often having little effect on eyesight but, if necessary, surgery is usually a successful treatment. Screening is available for this condition.

Entropion

This is an inherited eye condition which presents as an in-rolling of the eyelids. This ranges in severity from mild to the more serious, where surgical correction is required because of the pain and damage that is inflicted on the eyeball.

Generalised progressive retinal atrophy

This is a degenerative disease of the retina which presents as night blindness and progresses to a complete loss of vision.

Onset may be as young as two years of age, but is more commonly diagnosed at around four or five years. A DNA test is available which determines whether a dog is a carrier of this condition, as it is possible for a dog to be unaffected but produce affected offspring.

Goniodysgenesis/Primary glaucoma

This condition is also known as angle closure glaucoma and is caused by abnormal development of the eye whereby fluid is constantly produced but cannot drain away.

This results in increased pressure, damaging the retina and causing acute conjunctivitis and pain. Medication is available but surgery is often needed to relieve the pressure.

IMHA and IMTP

English Springers appear to have a predisposition to immune-mediated haemolytic anaemia (IMHA) and immune-mediated thrombocytopaenia (IMTP). The body's immune system sees the red blood cells

(IMHA) or platelets (IMTP) as foreign and destroys them. Signs range from mild to chronic anaemia, to life-threatening collapse. Both conditions can be treated with immune-suppressive medications, but repeated blood transfusions may be necessary in severe cases.

Joint disorders

Hip dysplasia

This is a malformation of the hip joint where the head of the femur does not align with the cup of the hip socket. Resulting lameness ranges from mild to severe. Surgery can be effective. All potential breeding stock should be x-rayed and hip-scored.

Incomplete ossification of the humeral condyle

This is a condition where the cartilage growth plate of the humerus (the bone from the shoulder to the elbow) fails to ossify and mature at the elbow joint. As a result there is a line of weakness and a fracture can occur with minimal stress, such as normal exercise. The first signs will be lameness in one or both forelimbs from a young age. Surgery may help to stablilise the joint but it is likely to be affected by osteoarthritis later in life.

Phosphofructokinase (PFK) deficiency

PFK is an enzyme that helps to convert sugar into energy in the cells. Deficiency causes low sugar levels which results in dark-coloured urine, pale gums, jaundice, fever and poor appetite, made worse after exercise. Symptoms range from mild to life threatening. There is no treatment but the condition can be managed by reducing stress and exercise. A DNA test is available to determine whether a dog is clear, affected or a carrier.

Summing up

It may give the pet owner cause for concern to find out about health problems that may affect their dog. But it is important to bear in mind that acquiring some basic knowledge is an asset, as it will allow you to spot signs of trouble at an early stage. Early diagnosis is very often the means to the most effective treatment.

Fortunately, the English Springer is a generally healthy and disease-free dog, with his only visits to the vet being annual check-ups. In most cases, owners can look forward to enjoying many happy years with this affectionate and highly entertaining companion.

Useful addresses

Breed & Kennel Clubs
Please contact your Kennel Club to obtain contact information about breed clubs in your area.

UK
The Kennel Club (UK)
1 Clarges Street London, W1J 8AB
Telephone: 0870 606 6750
Fax: 0207 518 1058
Web: www.thekennelclub.org.uk

USA
American Kennel Club (AKC)
5580 Centerview Drive, Raleigh, NC 27606.
Telephone: 919 233 9767
Fax: 919 233 3627
Email: info@akc.org
Web: www.akc.org

United Kennel Club (UKC)
100 E Kilgore Rd, Kalamazoo,
MI 49002-5584, USA.
Tel: 269 343 9020
Fax: 269 343 7037
Web:www.ukcdogs.com/

Australia
Australian National Kennel Council (ANKC)
The Australian National Kennel Council is the administrative body for pure breed canine affairs in Australia. It does not, however, deal directly with dog exhibitors, breeders or judges. For information pertaining to breeders, clubs or shows, please contact the relevant State or Territory Body.

International
Fédération Cynologique Internationalé (FCI)
Place Albert 1er, 13, B-6530 Thuin, Belgium.
Tel: +32 71 59.12.38
Fax: +32 71 59.22.29
Web: www.fci.be

Training and behavior
UK
Association of Pet Dog Trainers
Telephone: 01285 810811
Web: http://www.apdt.co.uk

Canine Behaviour
Association of Pet Behaviour Counsellors
Telephone: 01386 751151
Web: www.apbc.org.uk

USA
Association of Pet Dog Trainers
Tel: 1 800 738 3647
Web: www.apdt.com

American College of Veterinary Behaviorists
Web: www.dacvb.org

American Veterinary Society of Animal Behavior
Web: www.avsabonline.org

Australia
APDT Australia Inc
Web: www.apdt.com.au

For details of regional behaviorists, contact the relevant State or Territory Controlling Body.

Activities

UK

Agility Club
www.agilityclub.co.uk

British Flyball Association
Telephone: 01628 829623
Web: www.flyball.org.uk

USA

North American Dog Agility Council
Web: www.nadac.com

North American Flyball Association, Inc.
Tel/Fax: 800 318 6312
Web: www.flyball.org

Australia

Agility Dog Association of Australia
Tel: 0423 138 914
Web: www.adaa.com.au

NADAC Australia
Web: www.nadacaustralia.com

Australian Flyball Association
Tel: 0407 337 939
Web: www.flyball.org.au

International

World Canine Freestyle Organisation
Tel: (718) 332-8336
Web: www.worldcaninefreestyle.org

Health

UK

British Small Animal Veterinary Association
Tel: 01452 726700
Web: www.bsava.com

Royal College of Veterinary Surgeons
Tel: 0207 222 2001
Web: www.rcvs.org.uk

Alternative Veterinary Medicine Centre
Tel: 01367 710324
Web: www.alternativevet.org

USA

American Veterinary Medical Association
Tel: 800 248 2862
Web: www.avma.org

American College of Veterinary Surgeons
Tel: 301 916 0200
Toll Free: 877 217 2287
Web: www.acvs.org

Canine Eye Registration Foundation
The Veterinary Medical DataBases
1717 Philo Rd, PO Box 3007,
Urbana, IL 61803-3007
Tel: 217-693-4800
Fax: 217-693-4801
Web: www.vmdb.org/cerf

Orthopaedic Foundation of Animals
2300 E Nifong Boulevard
Columbia, Missouri, 65201-3806
Tel: 573 442-0418
Fax: 573 875-5073
Web: www.offa.org

American Holistic Veterinary Medical
Association
Tel: 410 569 0795
Web: www.ahvma.org

Australia

Australian Small Animal Veterinary
Association
Tel: 02 9431 5090
Web: www.asava.com.au

Australian Veterinary Association
Tel: 02 9431 5000
Web: www.ava.com.au

Australian College Veterinary Scientists
Tel: 07 3423 2016
Web: www.acvsc.org.au

Australian Holistic Vets
Web: www.ahv.com.au